Praise for *The Father of the Man*

"Beowulf Sheehan's fascinating double portrait of the great Cormac McCarthy in photographs and prose is also an autobiography. Difficult fathers and painful childhoods unite both men, and Sheehan, in revealing himself, helps us get under the guard of the famously reticent writer."
—Salman Rushdie

"Of course it would take an artist who sees what others do not to uncover the final story that this most reticent of authors had not planned to tell. Of course it also means that the window Sheehan encounters turns out to be a mirror where his own life, lineage and legacy leap into sharp and brilliant focus."
—Marlon James, author of *The Disappearers*, winner of the Man Booker Prize, and author of the introduction to Cormac McCarthy's *Blood Meridian: Or the Evening Redness in the West*

"Beowulf Sheehan is more than a photographer. He is a conduit through which his subjects become known to us. These extraordinary pictures of Cormac McCarthy reveal not only Sheehan's keen eye, but also his deep understanding of the man beneath his gaze, an understanding made possible by McCarthy's obvious openness to Sheehan, and Sheehan's empathy, experience, and humanity."
—Tracy Daugherty, author of *Cormac McCarthy: A Legacy Revisited*

"Over the last two decades, Beowulf Sheehan has become the definitive photographer of contemporary writers. Now, to accompany his definitive final portraits of Cormac McCarthy, and greatly deepen their context, he has given us a glimpse into his own story of becoming in a moving essay that lets us see just why he is so good at what he does. This brief, sumptuous book is a gem."
—Adam Haslett, author of the *Los Angeles Times* Book Prize-winning *Imagine Me Gone*

"Sheehan masterfully frames the propulsive and archetypal energy of the father wound, which so many of us—especially in the arts—nurse throughout our lives. Achingly real. Tantalizing. Wise. Beautiful. I devoured it."
—Matthew Quick, *New York Times* bestselling author of *The Silver Linings Playbook* and *Dad, Love, Me*

"*The Father of the Man* is a remarkably moving engagement with Cormac McCarthy, both visually and in Beowulf's painfully honest reflections on the way McCarthy's work made echoes in his own life. An exquisite book."
—Phil Klay, author of the National Book Award-winning *Redeployment*

"Beowulf is a kindhearted and compassionate storyteller. His moving words and pictures give us rare moments of pause and reflection on the life of the iconic artist Cormac McCarthy and how his art touches our lives."
—Platon, portrait photographer and winner of the World Press Photo Prize

"An intimate and moving reflection on how the art that speaks to us intersects with our lives, from an artist who is himself at the top of his form."
—Dr. Stacey Peebles, author of *Cormac McCarthy and Performance: Page, Stage, Screen*

"In both words and images, a fine and illuminating companion to McCarthy's work."
—*Kirkus Reviews*

The Father of the Man

The Last Author Portrait Sitting with Cormac McCarthy

Beowulf Sheehan

Autofocus Books
Easton, Pennsylvania

Published by Autofocus Books
autofocusbooks.com

Photography/Memoir
ISBN: 978-1-957392-49-3

Cover design by Amy Wheaton
Library of Congress Control Number: 2026938967

The Father of the Man

The Last Author Portrait Sitting
with Cormac McCarthy

Tuesday, June 24, 2014. I'm on the phone with Binky Urban, literary agent for the likes of Toni Morrison, Haruki Murakami, and Cormac McCarthy. Happy with my photographs of Donna Tartt for *The Goldfinch* a year earlier, Binky offers me the opportunity to work with Cormac. I share the great news with Nicholas Latimer, publicity director of Cormac's publisher Alfred A. Knopf, and, following dialogue with Binky and Nicholas, an introductory call with Cormac is scheduled.

Cormac famously believed that "if [the story] doesn't concern life and death, it's not interesting." The works of his I'd read by this time (*All the Pretty Horses, Blood Meridian, The Road,* and *The Stonemason*) were, by his measure, interesting, but they interested me for different reasons. At this stage of my life (and I hope, dear reader, at this stage of yours), I find that every book I read has something in it that speaks to my life and, therefore, to me. The story is "interesting" to me because I feel connected to it.

In his work, Cormac often wove threads between fathers and sons: a son's love for a father and a father's love for a son, the dissolution and resolution of the two. These are the threads that connect his stories to mine.

[ ]

At 11am on Tuesday, July 22, I sit on the floor of my studio, alone. Having read and seen what interviews with Cormac McCarthy I could find online, I'm excited. And nervous. I calm my breathing and dial the number.

Cormac answers. He is courteous, drawn, measured. I tell him I'm honored for the opportunity, and he says the same. I ask him to tell me what he can about *The Passenger.* I didn't know at the time, of course, that one novel would become two (in the forms of *The Passenger* and *Stella Maris*) and that the two wouldn't publish for another eight years. Usually, I ask the writers I photograph if I may read their forthcoming books before their sessions. This time, I don't. Binky had advised me not to. Cormac says his book is about a woman with synesthesia. To varying degrees, both he and his son John have the condition. Cormac notes that the novel is, among other things, an exercise in exploring it.

I compliment Cormac on the success of the film adaptation of *No Country for Old Men*. He responds that being on set was "fun." I ask him to share his thoughts on contemporary film and books, and he says that he doesn't talk much about books, but he does love movies. He offers that his favorite movie is *Five Easy Pieces.* "It spoke to me."

I ask Cormac if he has any vision or special wishes for his author portrait. He tells me only what he doesn't want: "Nothing in the weeds."

[ ]

A few nights later, I watch *Five Easy Pieces*. In the film, Jack Nicholson's protagonist Bobby Dupea works on a California oil rig while his father Nicholas declines in Washington State. Unbeknownst to Bobby's co-workers, Nicholas had raised him to become a prodigal pianist. It's a career and a relationship from which Bobby runs until he learns from his sister that his father is near death. Bobby visits his father to make one last attempt at making peace.

Toward the end of the film, to his wheelchair-bound, mute father, Bobby acknowledges that there had always been distance and discomfort between them. He apologizes for not becoming the person his father wanted him to be.

Binky once told me that Cormac had said of *The Road*, "This is my life."

Our connection is clear.

[ ]

My father left my life when I was ten. Seated next to our mother in my bedroom, he announced to my brother and me that they were getting a divorce. My brother and I cried. Then my brother went into his room and punched the walls. After my mom and dad left my bedroom, I stared silently at my books. I was not a physical kid. I didn't like sports, or even recess or P.E. class due to my asthma, but in books I could do things nobody on the kickball field could.

I didn't hear from my father for three years after the divorce. From my young perspective, the years were hard on my mother, left alone to fend for herself, my brother, and me. I didn't learn to cook, but I did odd jobs and helped her as best I could. She tried to find a father figure for me through Big Brothers Big Sisters. I met a few potential "bigs," as they're called, but I didn't connect with anyone. I passed a lot of time bicycling to the Broward County Public Library, reading away.

When I was thirteen and a high school freshman, a card arrived in the mail. An invitation to a housewarming nearby. My father's new house, one mile from mine. My brother and I attended. The only other guest was a woman our father was dating. I remember wanting to ask why he disappeared, why he didn't pay child support. I wanted to learn who he was, but I said nothing. Here was the man who took my brother and me to the beach, to school, to my first movie, whose penmanship matched that of Santa's note by the tree on Christmas morning, who I saw assault my mother during their divorce proceedings. Who I wanted to learn to trust and love anew.

During a later visit, a picture was made: my father and I on the dock behind his house. (Some houses in Fort Lauderdale had docks behind them and had boats connected to those docks. Sometimes my father's house had both.) In the photograph, he held a camera and I smiled, my body listing slightly away from him, my fingers curled inward.

[ ]

I know nothing of Cormac's relationship with his own father, Charles, who had worked as an attorney in Knoxville. Nothing, except what he tells his readers through his novels. *The Orchard Keeper,* Cormac's debut novel published in 1965, is about a son who meets a bootlegger who, unbeknownst to the son, has murdered his father. *Outer Dark,* his second, is a horror story of an infant born of incest, taken to the woods to be killed but, though the father claims to have killed the child, is left alive and alone. In *Suttree,* the protagonist rejects his father and the comforts granted by him, then later rejects his wife, child, and society in favor of life without construct on the Tennessee River. In *Blood Meridian*, an orphan described only as "the kid" is overwhelmed by the brutality all around him, including his own. In *All the Pretty Horses,* the first book of *The Border Trilogy*, the ideals and searches of youth for purpose, place, and love confront systems and violence meant to silence if not end them. *No Country for Old Men* studies the consequence of chance, the evil men do for money, and a man who would stop that evil reflecting on his father who didn't stop for him. In *The Road*, humanity begets the apocalypse.

In its aftermath, as death comes for survivors, a father loves a son enough to implore him to keep going.

[ ]

When my father returned to my neighborhood and my life, he bought my brother and me things to win our favor, but I was most drawn to his camera atop a chest of drawers. My journey to engaging the world with a camera in hand was taking a step forward. As a boy, I had watched with fascination as my maternal grandfather made pictures of the family with a decades-old camera. I'd pored over prints at my grandparents' house. This attraction to my father's camera was different. I borrowed and began using it to document life and to meet people.

My father, more present as my high school years came to a close, didn't care for my interest in a career in art at the time. At his behest, I went on to earn an undergraduate degree I didn't want. I understood the role of finance in the world, but finding my role in the world of finance for the rest of my life didn't appeal to me. The companies named in a *South Florida Business Journal* article about commercial photographers from Europe who were driving the renaissance of Miami Beach, however, did. I read the article while waiting to interview at a bank. After failing the interview, I returned home to write to all the companies named in the article. Two weeks later, I had a small desk on Ocean Drive. I worked for a modeling agency, introducing me to photographers from around the world. Some weekends, I sculpted at the South Florida Arts Center, occasionally photographing models as studies for my sculpture. At night, I often read books from Books & Books on Lincoln Road.

Determined to find my place in the arts, I left home for New York four years after arriving in Miami Beach. Through my graduate studies at NYU, I interned at museums, magazines, and galleries. I helped sell a

Picasso. I later studied further at the International Center of Photography and ran a lecture series at the Camera Club of New York. With a full-time job in the fashion industry paying the bills and keeping me fed, I printed or photographed nights and weekends for six years. In 2003, my father sent me a copy of Helmut Newton's *Autobiography.* Inside it he inscribed, "To Beo - Christmas 2003 – I have taken the liberty of reading this book prior to sending it to you. It has given me a wider understanding of your quest! Best of luck! All my love, Dad." My last day behind another person's desk was November 4, 2004. I reached out to some connections in the fashion community and, to my relief, began to get work. The work taught me plenty, especially the lesson that my photographic voice was better suited for a different community.

My father saw the love I had for photography and all it gave me in return. He accepted and supported it, even if only with words in a letter. Words I'd longed to read. A step Bobby Dupea's father was presumed to not have taken in *Five Easy Pieces*. A step, I'd later read, Bobby Western's father was also presumed to not have taken in *The Passenger.*

Through Cormac's work, I considered my relationship with my father. I ventured answers to questions surrounding his disappearance, his distance, his denials. I strove to understand the challenges my father bore to live and love. I deepened in my complicated love for him. I wondered what more I might learn by soon working with Cormac.

[ ]

Tuesday, August 12. My photo assistant Chika and I arrive at the Santa Fe Institute, Cormac's home away from home, and load equipment into the library. Cormac is early, chatting up the kitchen staff. We introduce ourselves. Cormac is perhaps 5'6" tall, and I'm 6'2", but his beaming "pleased to meet you" makes the greater impression on everyone in the room as he shakes our hands. Before we proceed to the library, I note the daylight coming through a side window. Cormac understands and obliges. He is as kind and accommodating in person as I hoped he'd be when we first spoke three Tuesdays before.

The sun is hard and coarse. In an adjoining courtyard, I mention the mystery and drama I see in the play of light and shadow there, and I ask Cormac if he's open to being part of it. Yes. And how. My banter with Cormac focuses on the institute, what compels him to be here. "My friends are here. We love the same things. We argue." What draws him to science? "It's fun." What drew him to Santa Fe? "It's home." We walk to and work in different corners of the library. Beyond the library is a balcony, and beyond it a nearly open sky. I invite Cormac to step to the balcony's edge and take in "home."

At our last institute location, a long exterior wall of adobe apart from its entrance, Cormac finally offers more: "Do you know the story of my typewriter?" No, I reply, just in case the story he's about to tell is different from the one I know. He tells Chika and me that he donated his Olivetti Lettera 32 typewriter to an auction to benefit the Santa Fe Institute. It fetched $250,000. A friend then went on eBay and bought a new one for him for a few dollars. A proud smile rests on Cormac's face. It might not have come if I'd said yes.

"Do you want to come to my house and make more pictures?"

I can't wait. We pack while Cormac retreats to his friends.

[ ]

Cormac's truck is weathered, rusted, dinged, easy to find in a crowd. We follow him through the traffic lights and intersections, out to where street-lights turn into street signs and abutted buildings turn into yarded homes. Farther still, as the road straightens and lengthens, the view is of open space. Then, on the right, a two-story, perhaps 4,000-square-foot adobe house rises into view. Numerous vehicles sit sprawled under tarps across his dusty driveway and land. Following Cormac's lead outside, I ask him about the cars he's collected. Pointing to one, he says, "That's a Corvette Stingray. I drove it back after I partied with Johnny Carson in Fort Lauderdale," laughing to himself. My hometown.

Inside, in the middle of his grand living room, stands a pristine billiards table. Of course, I think. That he financed his way through his early life by playing pool is lore. I don't ask about the table, and he doesn't offer comment. Instead, he invites Chika and me upstairs. The wash of Cormac's stairwell walls is as beautiful as an Irving Penn backdrop cloth. I photograph him along it, the sun pouring through his skylight, defining the space about him, redefining the shape of his face. Atop the stairs, Cormac asks what we think of the home so far, already knowing our answers. I ask him to stand strong and tall like the columns before him. After a few frames, he invites us to his bedroom, but first he wants to show us his son's room.

[ ]

Though Cormac doesn't name its occupant, the room is obviously John's. John, Cormac's younger son, was born in 1999. He was fifteen at the time of our session. (Cormac's older son Cullen was born in 1962, making him 51 or 52 at the time of our session.) The room is immaculate, the colorful bedding made, toy cars on shelves, an airplane hanging from the ceiling. The room appears frozen in time. I don't ask questions about either son.

Cormac's room is minimal, the bed perpendicular to the window, a stack of car magazines atop one bedside table, a lamp and radio atop the other, a set of plastic drawers holding papers on a bevel on the wall behind it, a guitar on the ground. Cormac's "new" Olivetti rests on the bed. "There it is," he says, pointing to the crate. "It" is *The Passenger,* a stack of papers typed on the Olivetti. On the opposite end of the otherwise empty bedside wall are the words "The Passenger" in large script, written by Cormac. With Cormac's consent, Chika opens the drapes. He moves his guitar and a few pillows on the floor. I ask him to stand before his window and give thought to the story he's crafted in this room. I invite him to sit with his typewriter. At each request, Cormac says nothing more than "Okay."

Downstairs, having seen most of the home, it occurs to me there's no television here. No stereo. No internet. There is, however, that great pool table, and on opposite sides of it there are tall, wall-length bookshelves. I ask Cormac to rest against them. Along the way I compliment him on his vast book collection. I venture that he must really love literature. Cormac is quick to correct me: "No, I love science." I misstep. "But I saw you had a number of books by Beckett on the shelf." "Beckett and Shakespeare. The rest," he says in so many words, raising his voice suddenly and surprisingly, "is science." I apologize for not reading his books' titles thoroughly, adding there are too many to note quickly.

"That's alright," Cormac replies. Just as suddenly and surprisingly, a light smile grows on his face. "You know, I had my son with me on the set of *No Country for Old Men*, on the day they blew some stuff up… the explosion was terrific. He thought it was the greatest thing ever." As I acknowledge this unprompted moment of love and pride, Cormac's smile turns into a laugh. It dawns on me that, from Cormac's perspective, our session might be an occasion for him to reflect on better moments of his life.

I think about Cullen. I think about John.

[ ]

Outside, I add film to our day of otherwise thus-far digital capture. "Why?" Cormac asks. "We might look different in different media," I answer. "So why not?" The dance between digital and film follows Cormac's dance between expressions, between dark and bright.

In his kitchen, the one modern end of his home, pots and pans hang from the ceiling, copper, gleaming, unmarked. We are in a small, adjacent nook, daylight falling on and fading from Cormac, both glints of joy and hints of ire showing through his eyes. I sense that our time together is drawing to a close. Cormac grants a picture with Chika. Then Chika makes a picture of Cormac and me. Cormac is as my father would largely be that year, after alcoholism constricted his life and before Alzheimer's ended it: smiling and saying little but very much engaged, happy to have my company. And now our time is done.

[ ]

Sometime into our drive back to Santa Fe, Chika and I come to a residential intersection. A truck revs into a quick turn as we wait at the stop sign. The driver is Cormac McCarthy. In that moment, our session behind us, we see Cormac as most do, if they see him at all: briefly, in passing, his writing the only means by which to take a good, long, appreciative look.

All history present in that visage, the child the father of the man.
—*Blood Meridian*

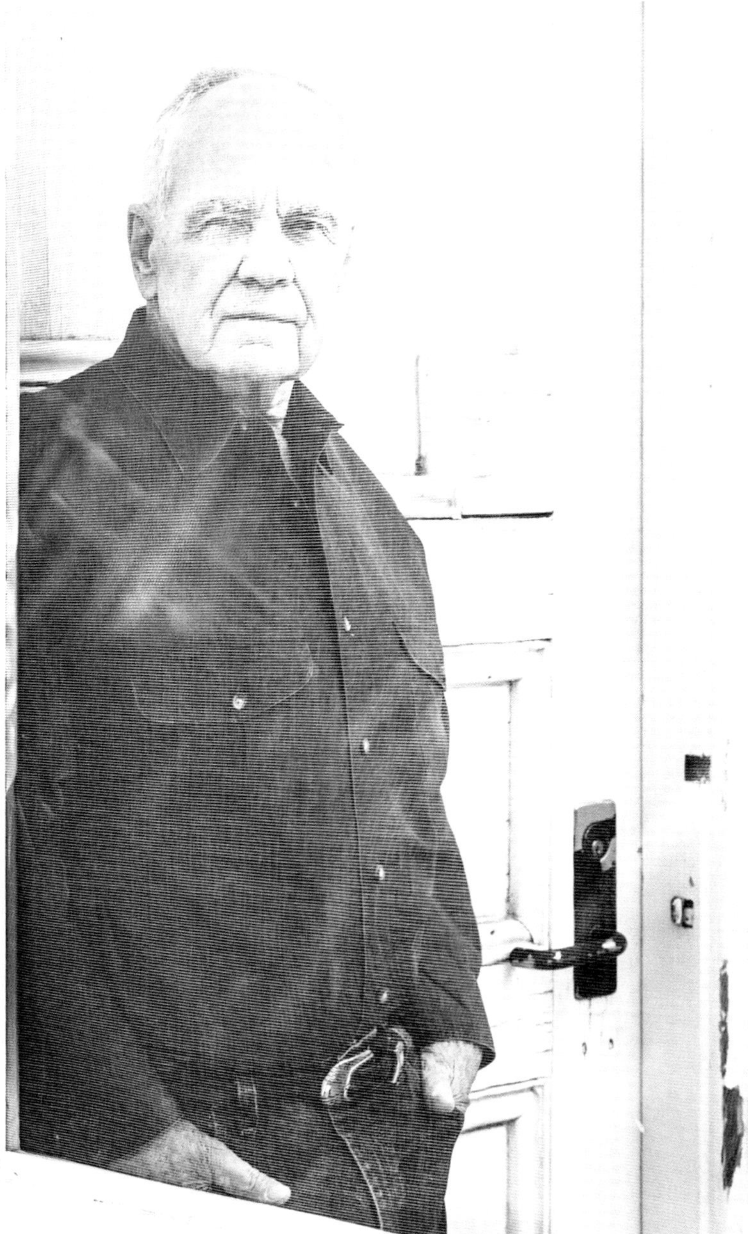

For we are all the elect, each one of us, and we are embarked upon a journey to something unimaginable. We do not know what will be required of us, and we have nothing to sustain us but the counsel of our fathers.

—*The Stonemason*

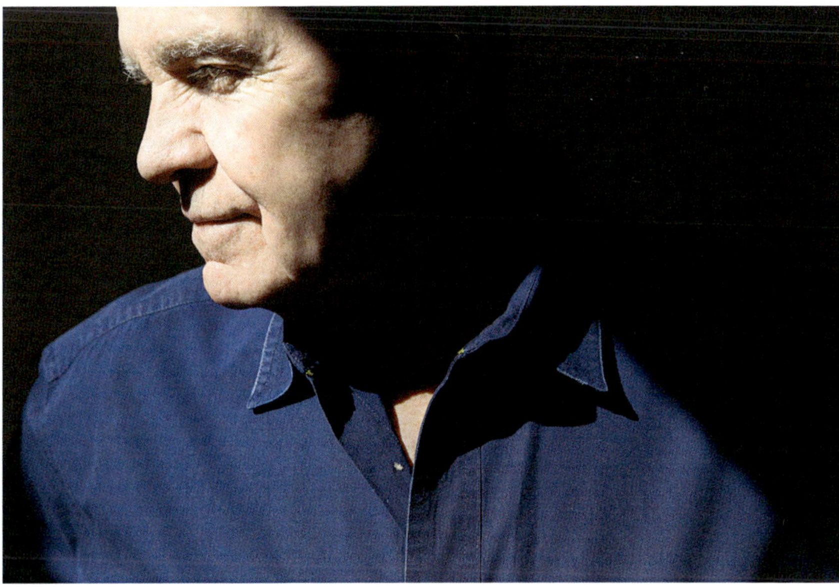

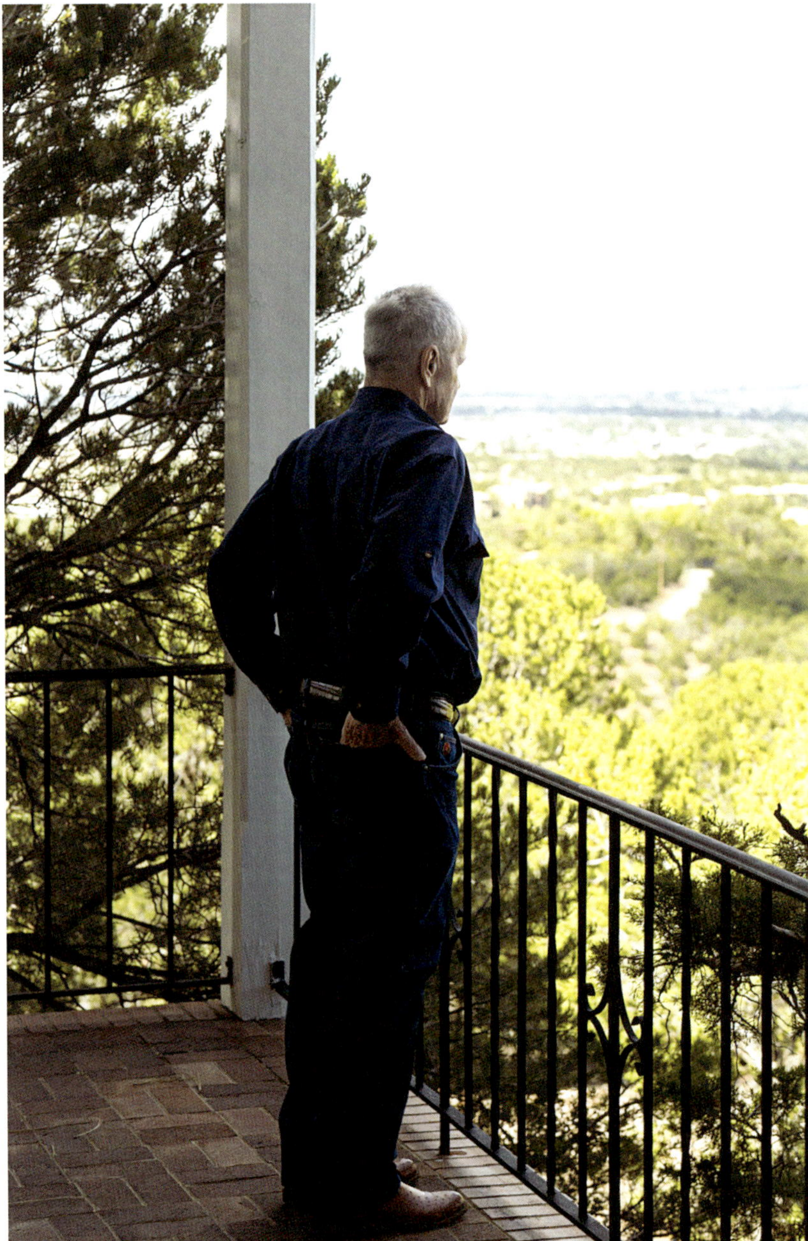

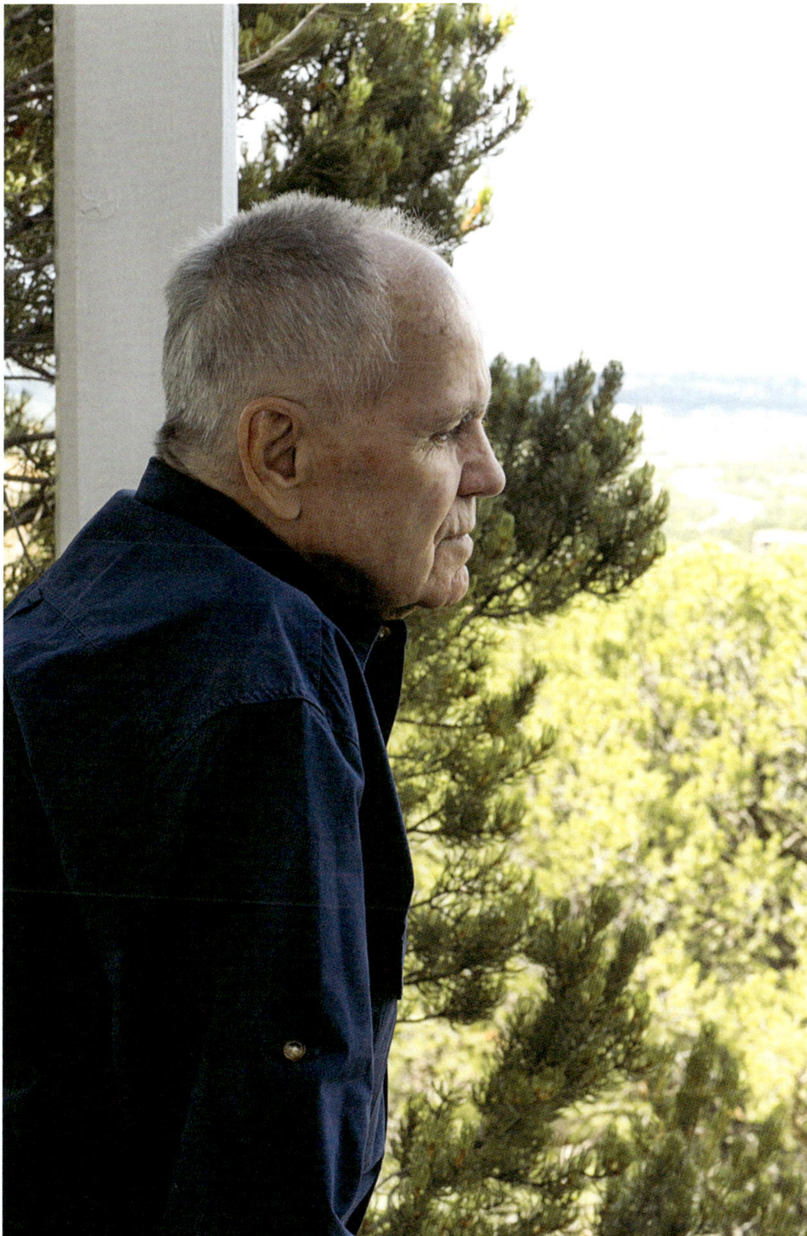

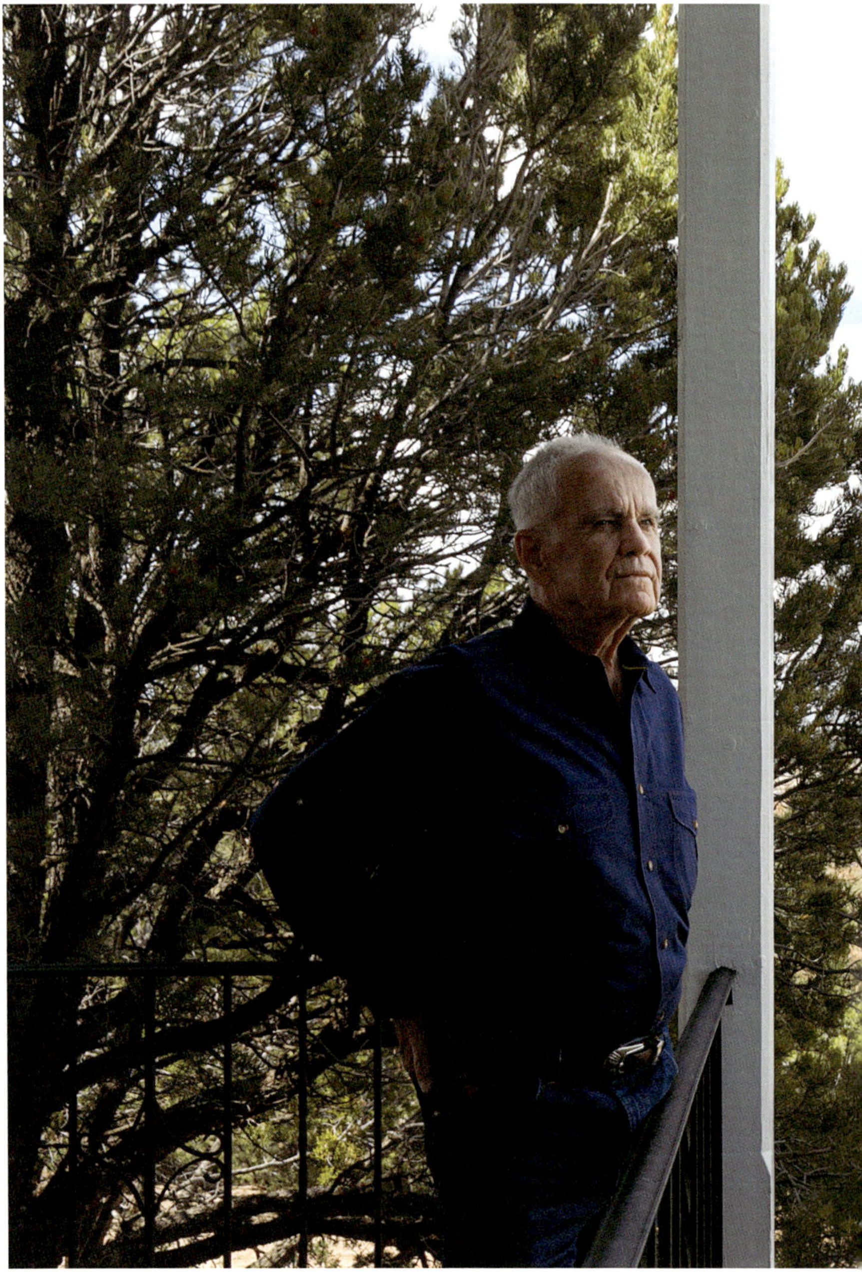

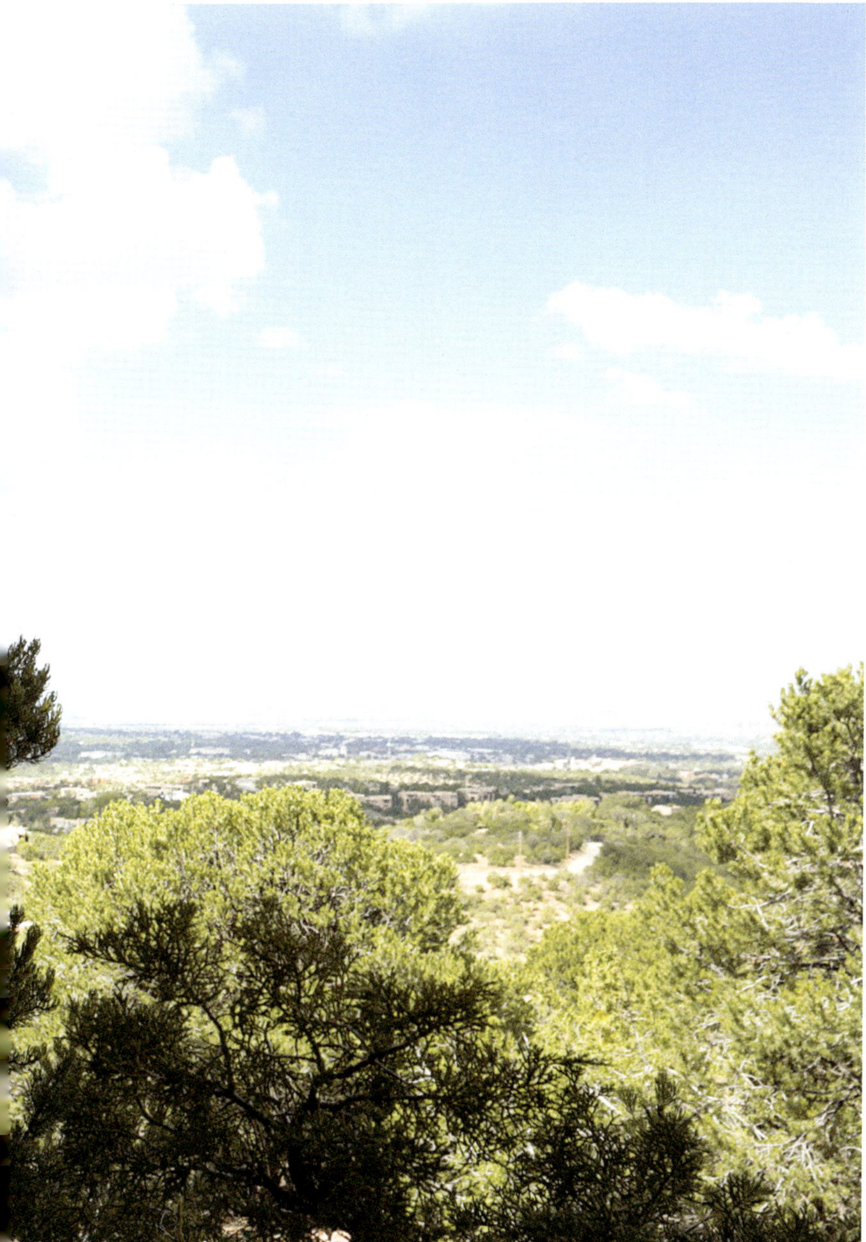

The rage of children seemed inexplicable other than as a breach of some deep and innate covenant having to do with how the world should be and wasnt.

How would a child know how the world should be?

A child would have to be born so.

—*Stella Maris*

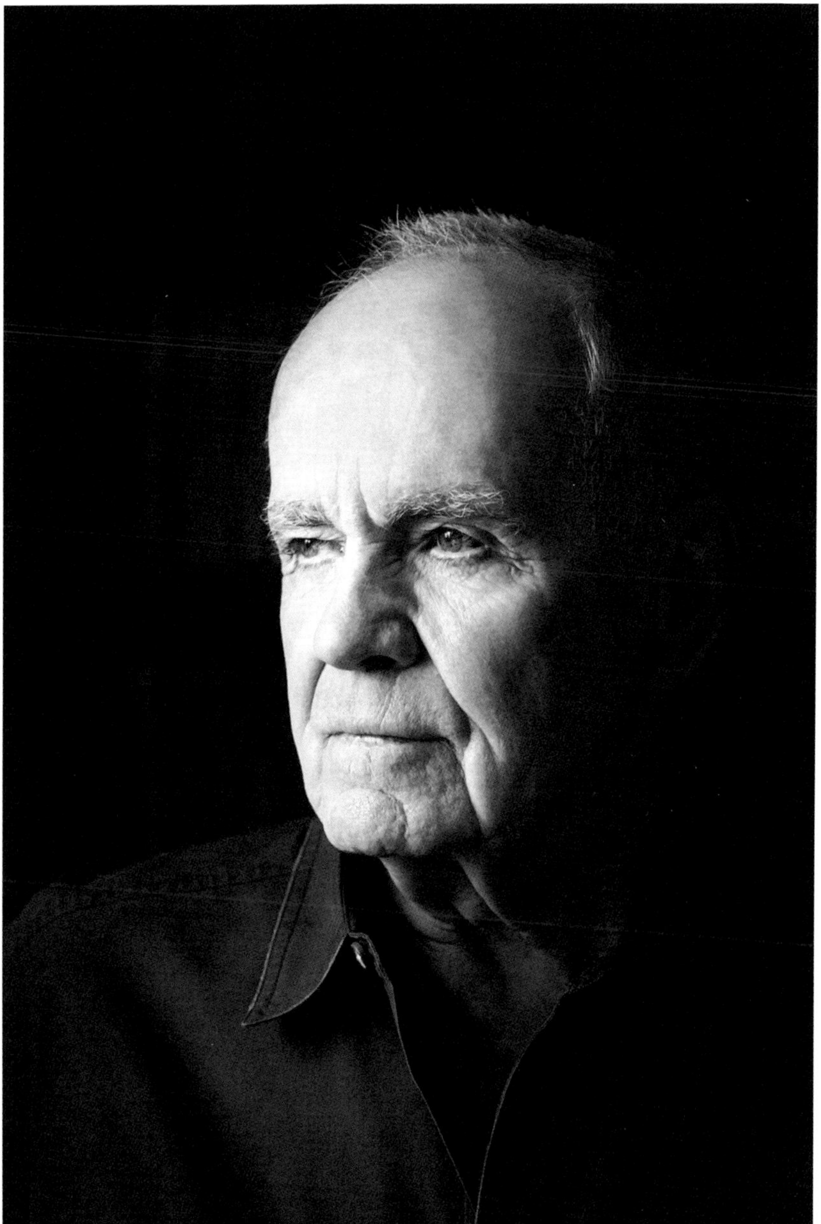

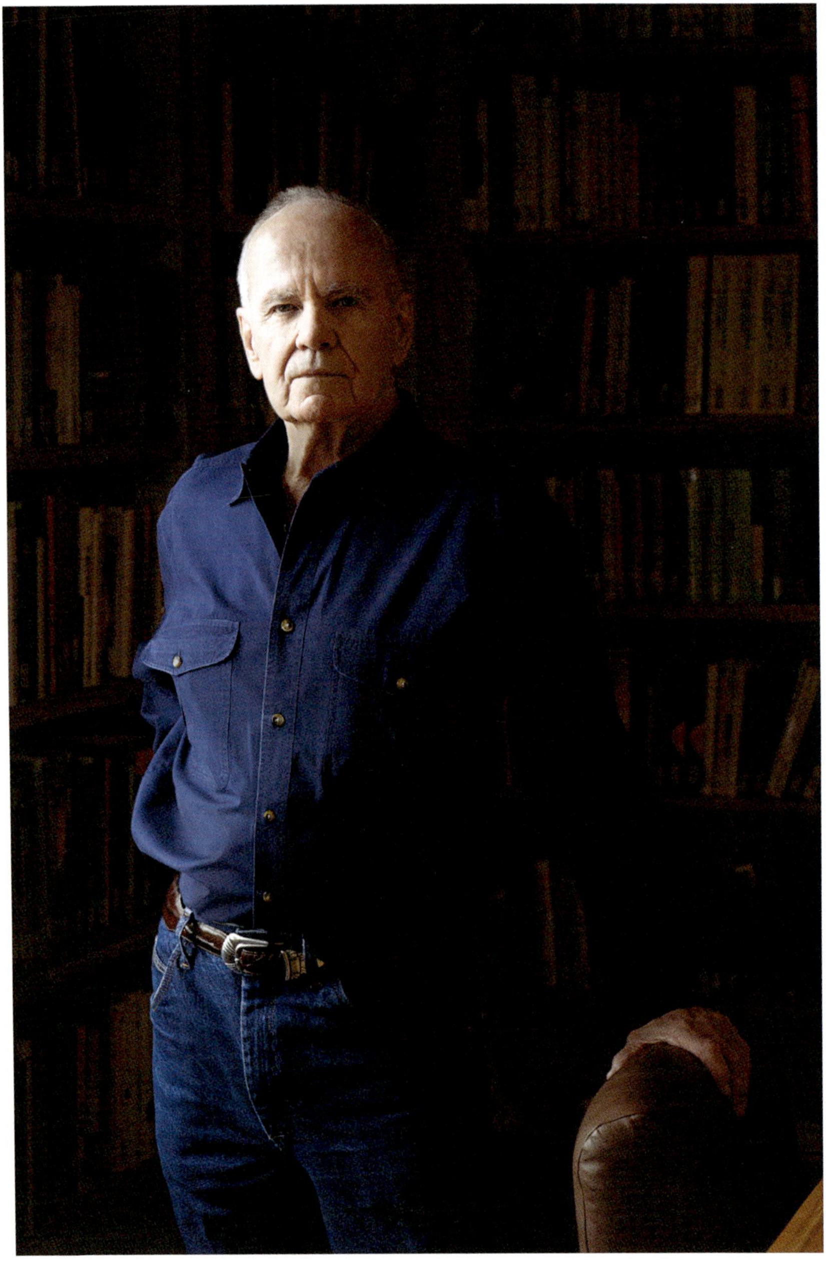

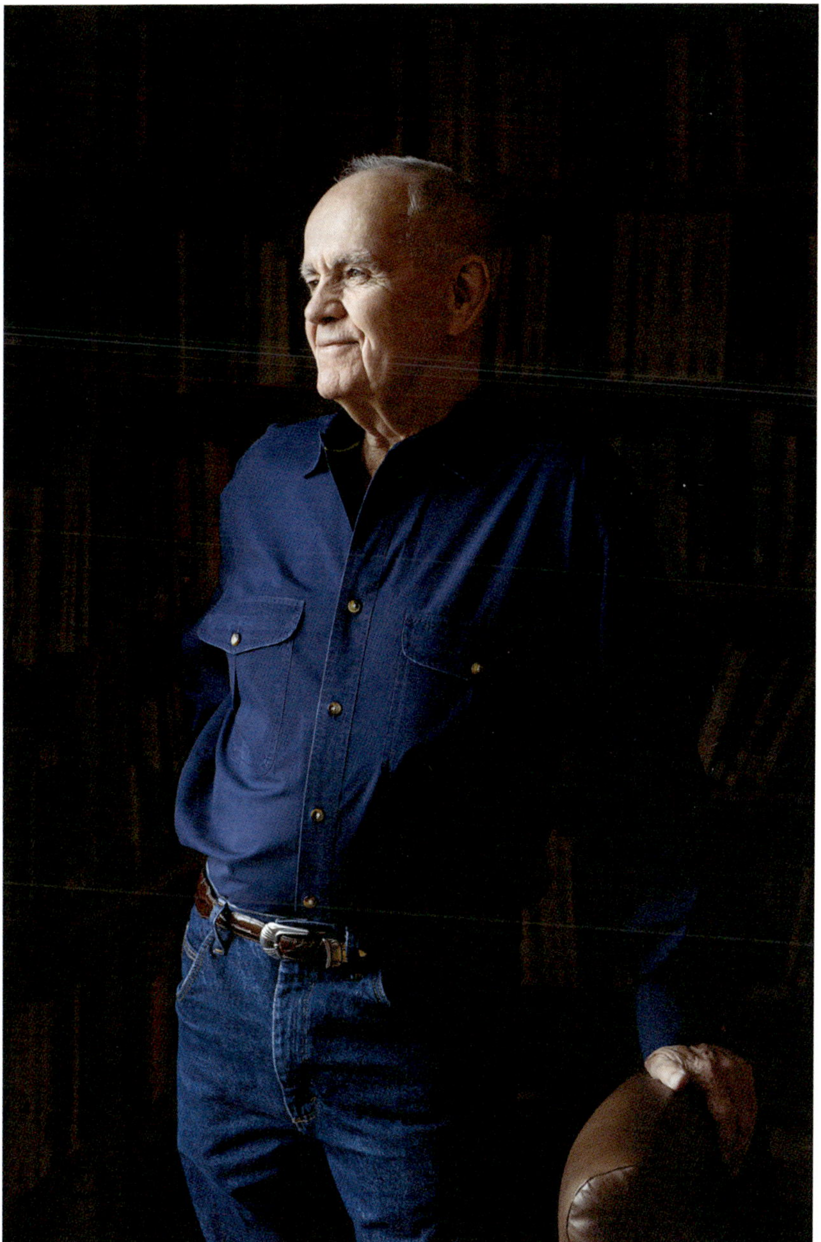

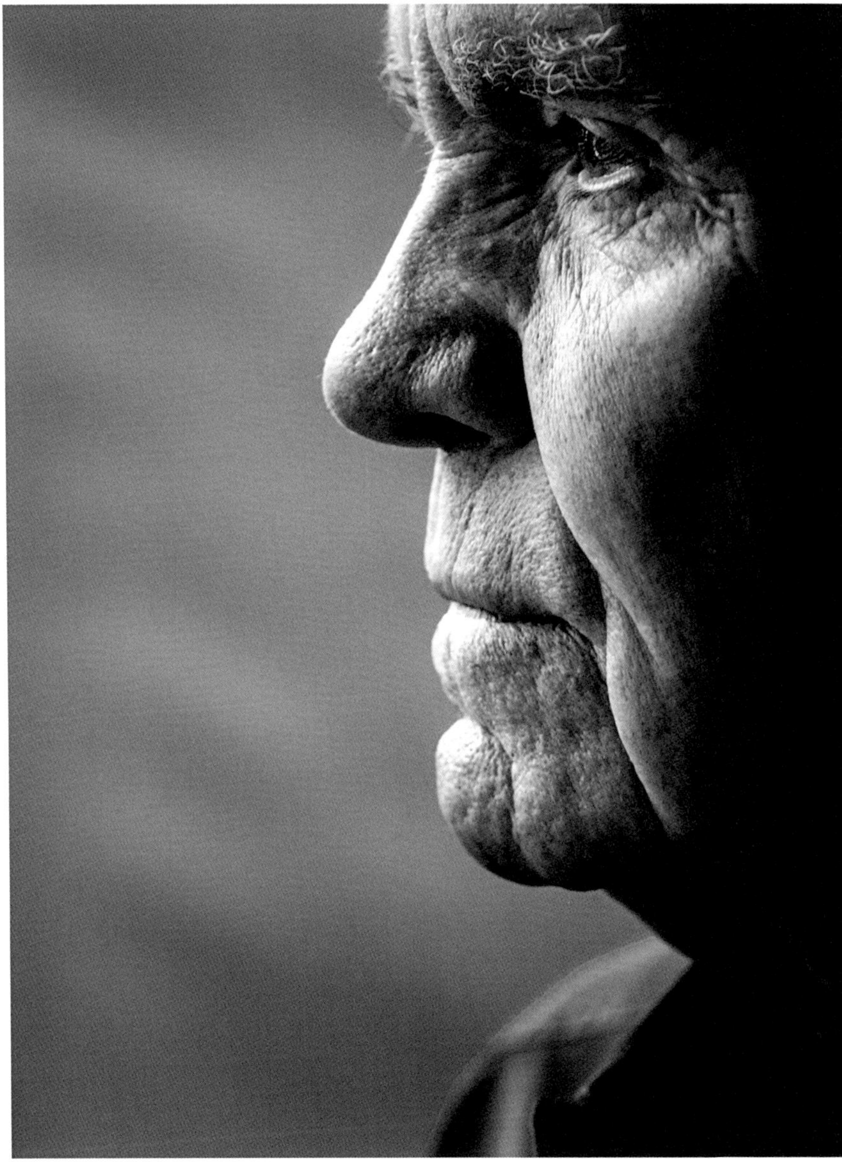

And in the dream I knew that [my father] was goin on ahead
and that he was fixin to make a fire somewhere out there
in all that dark and all that cold, and I knew that whenever
I got there he would be there. And then I woke up.
—No Country for Old Men

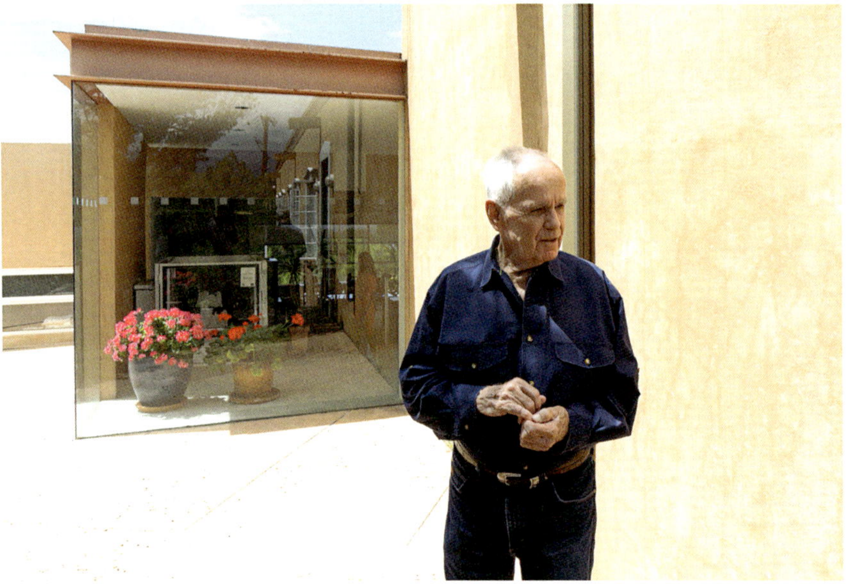

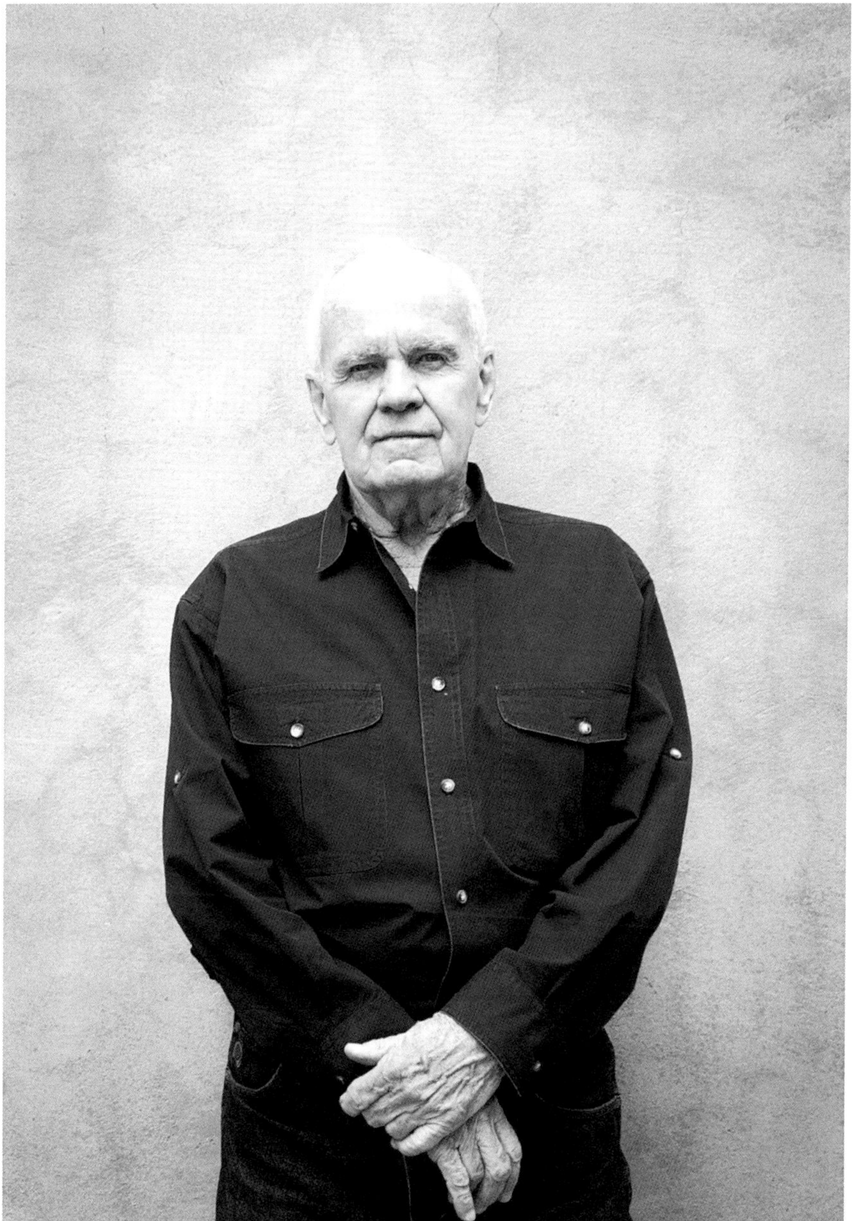

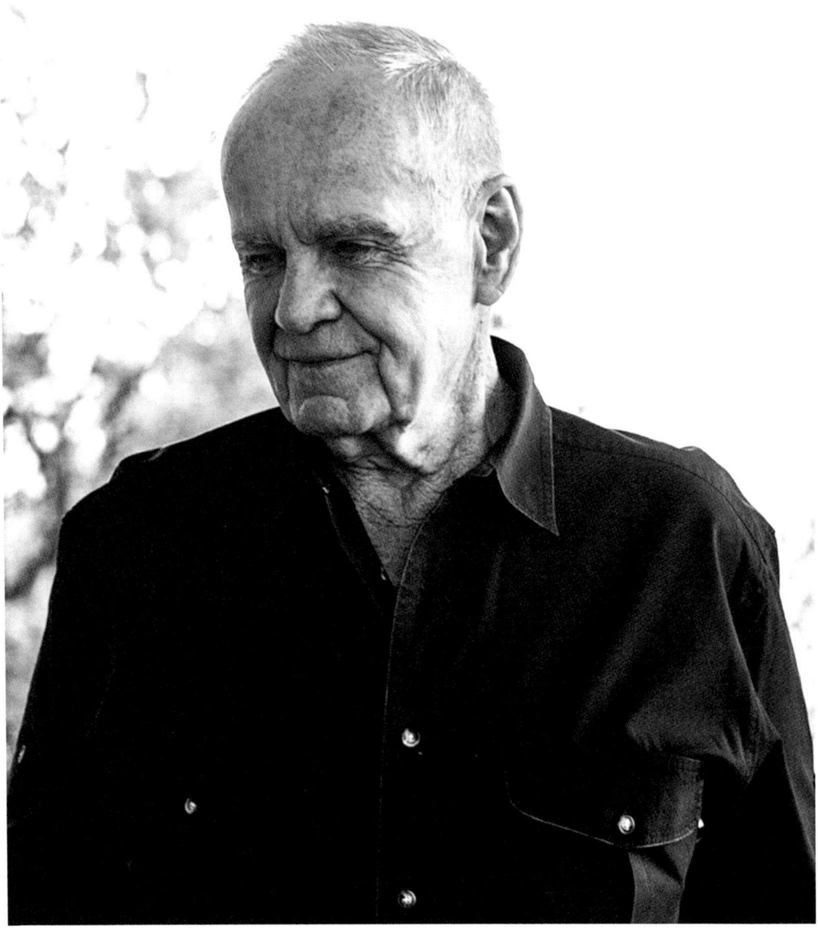

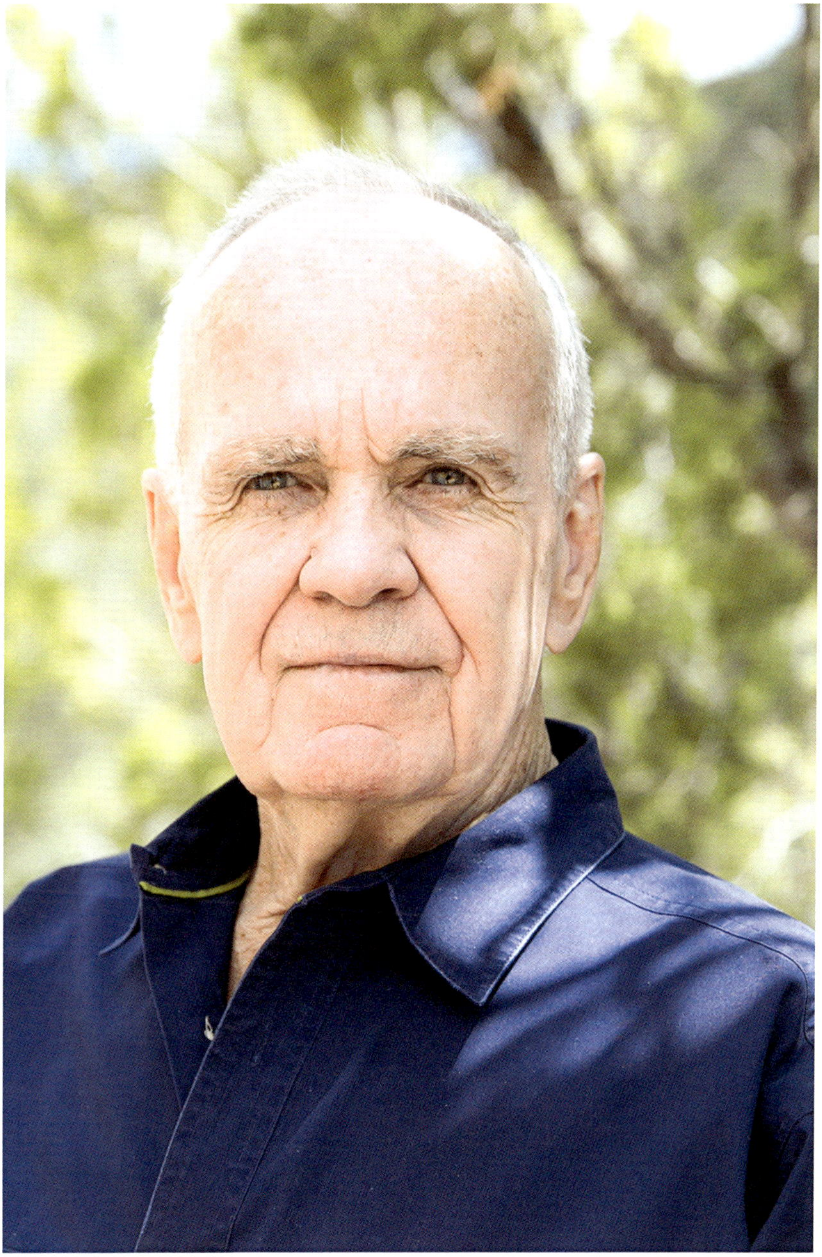

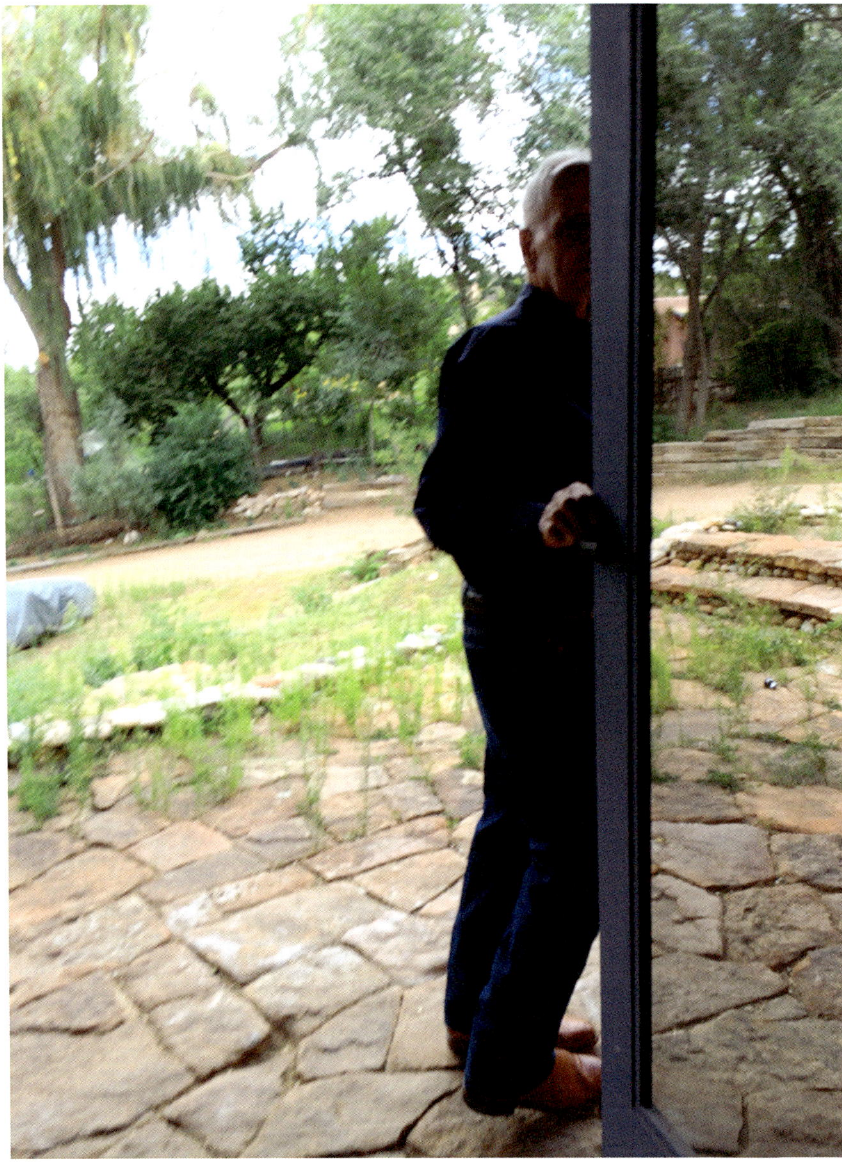

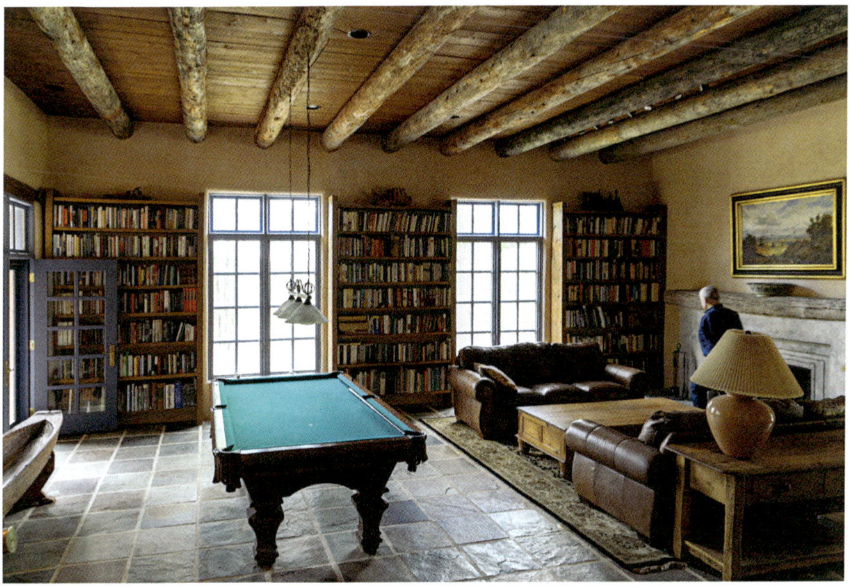

He knew only that the child was his warrant. He said:
If he is not the word of God God never spoke.
—*The Road*

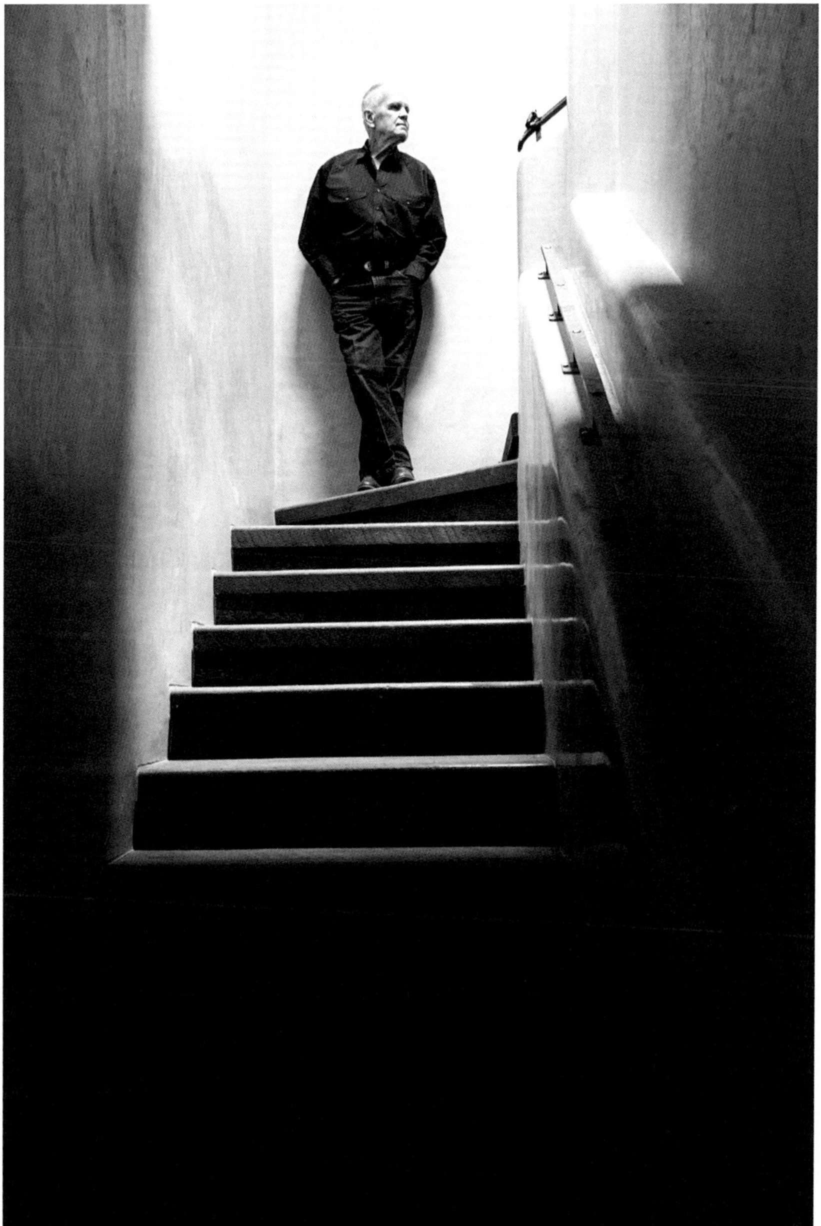

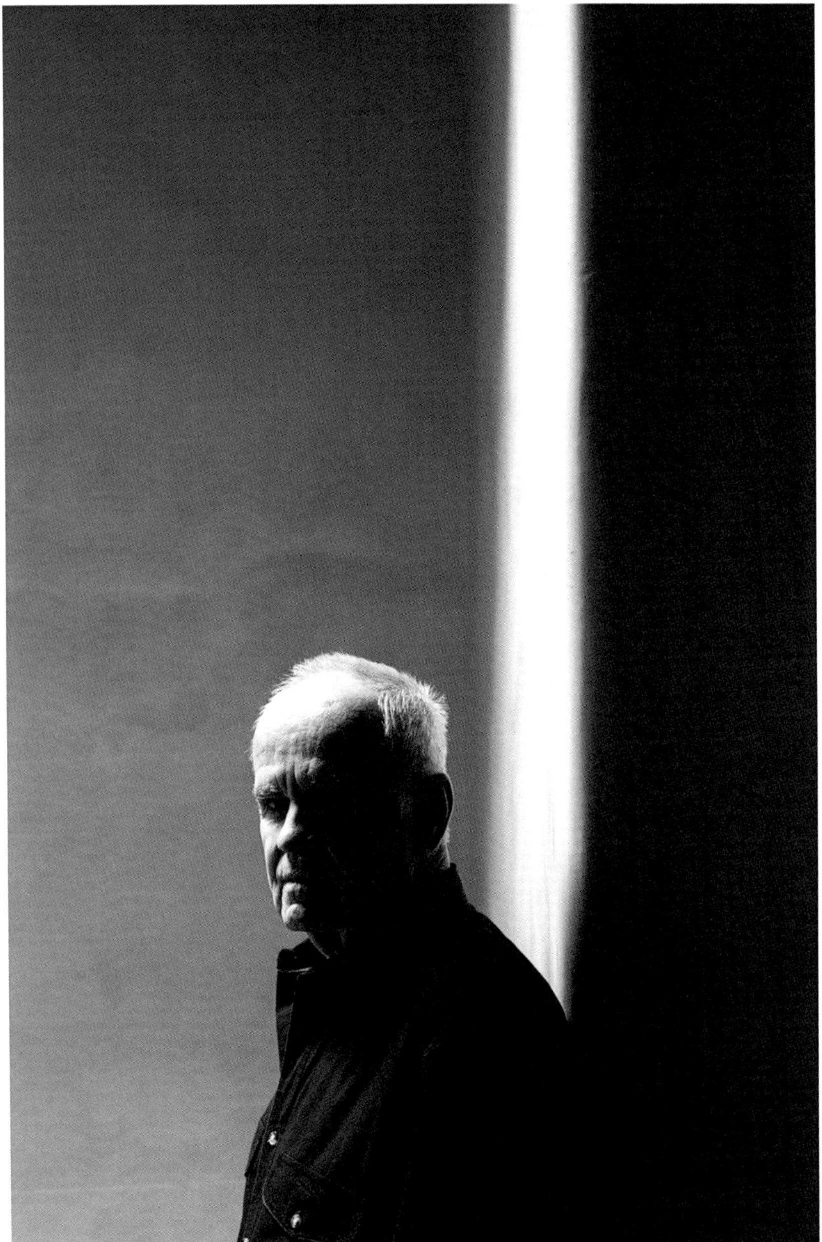

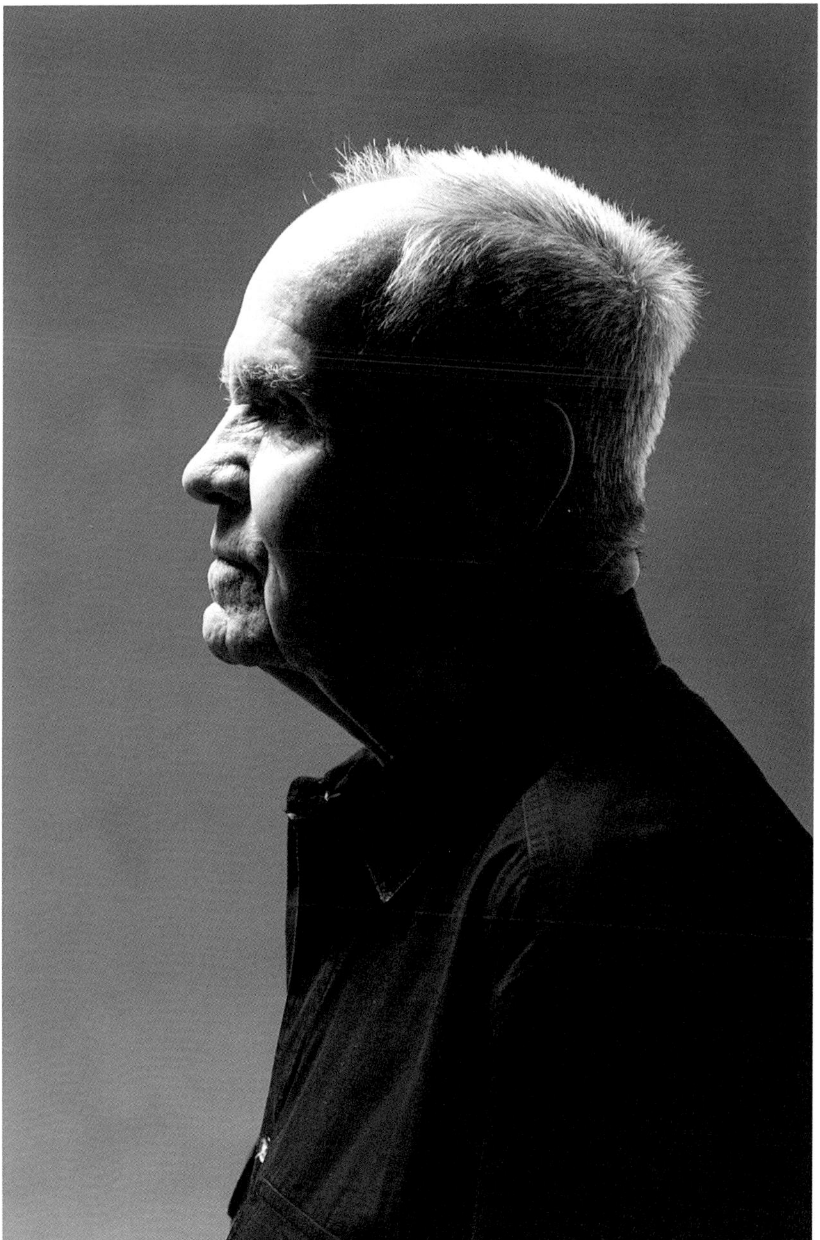

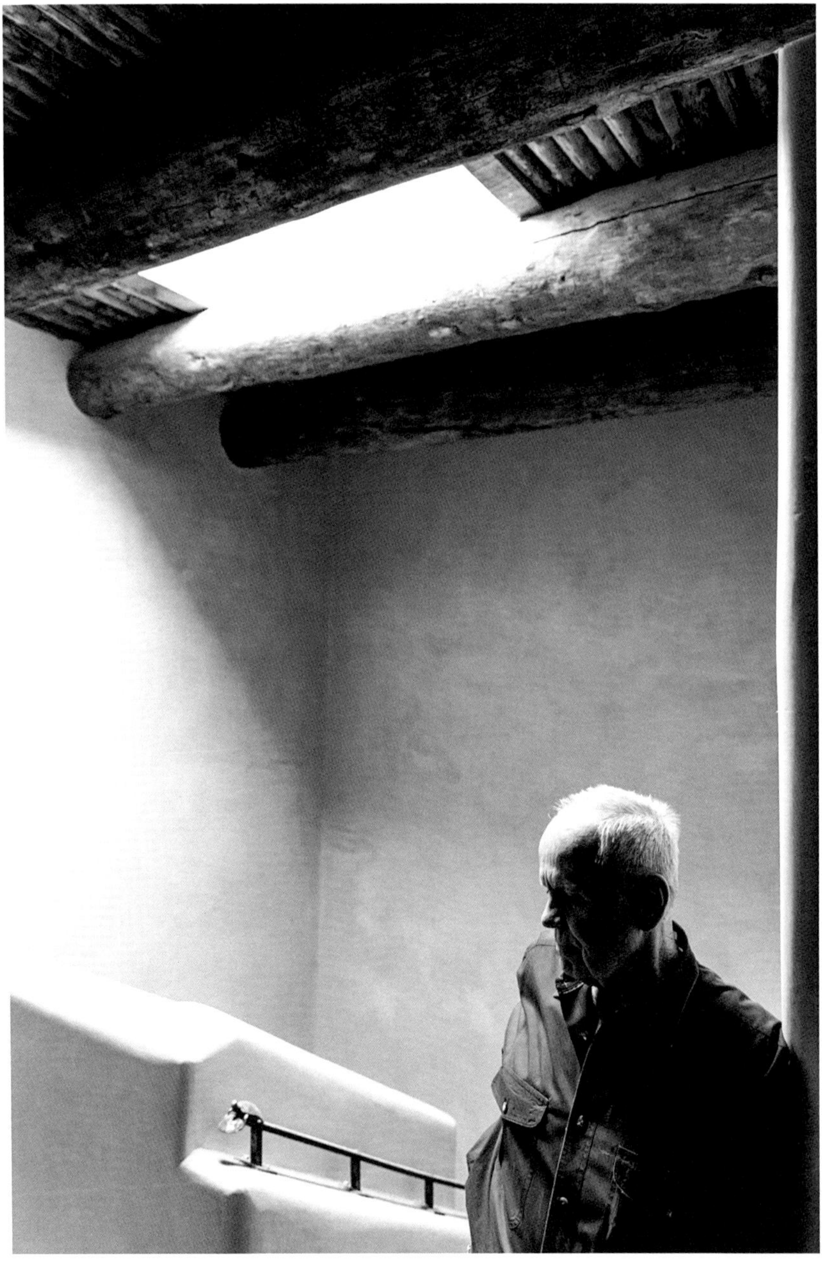

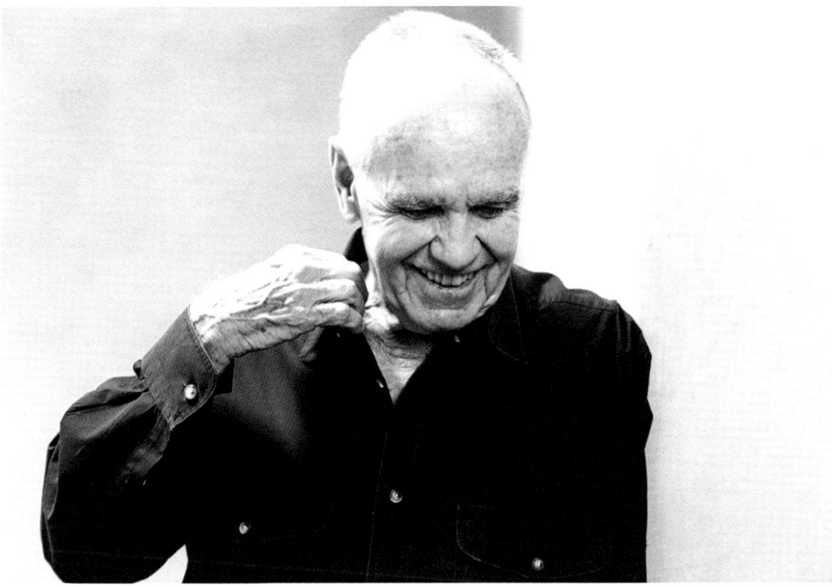

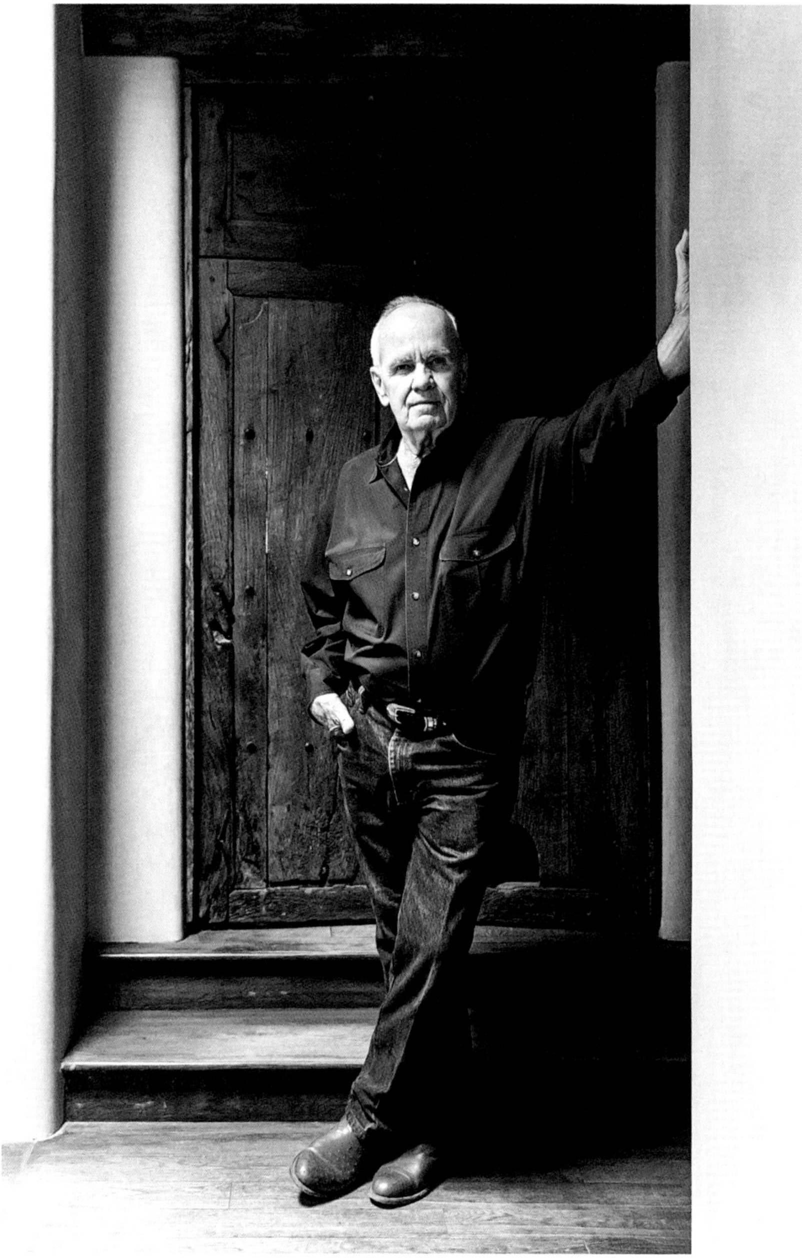

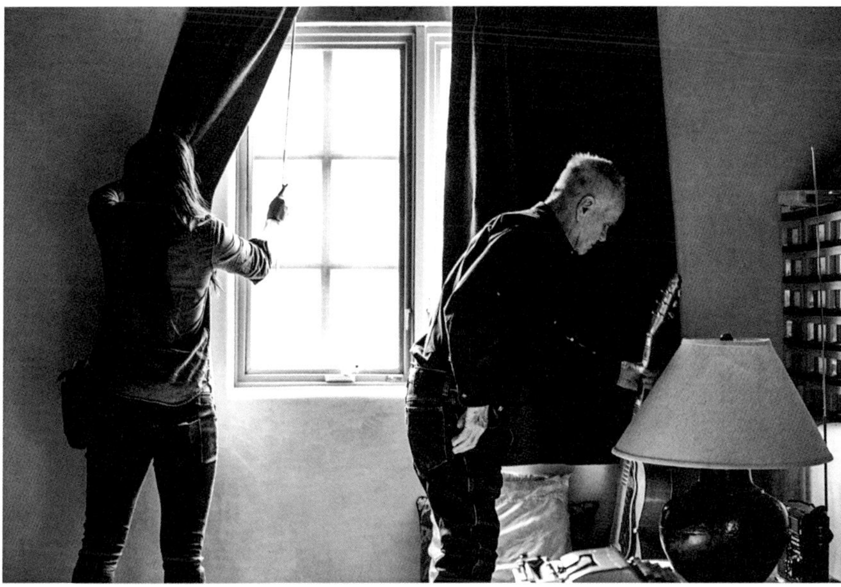

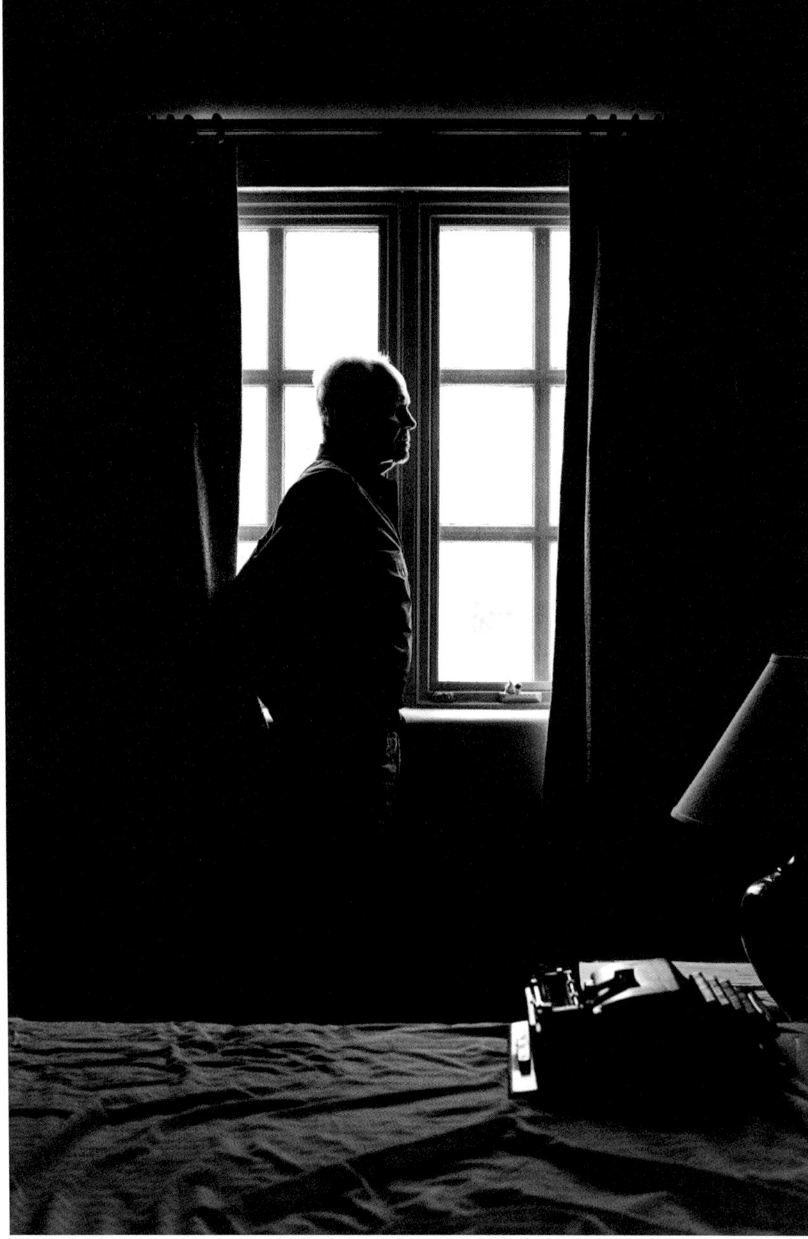

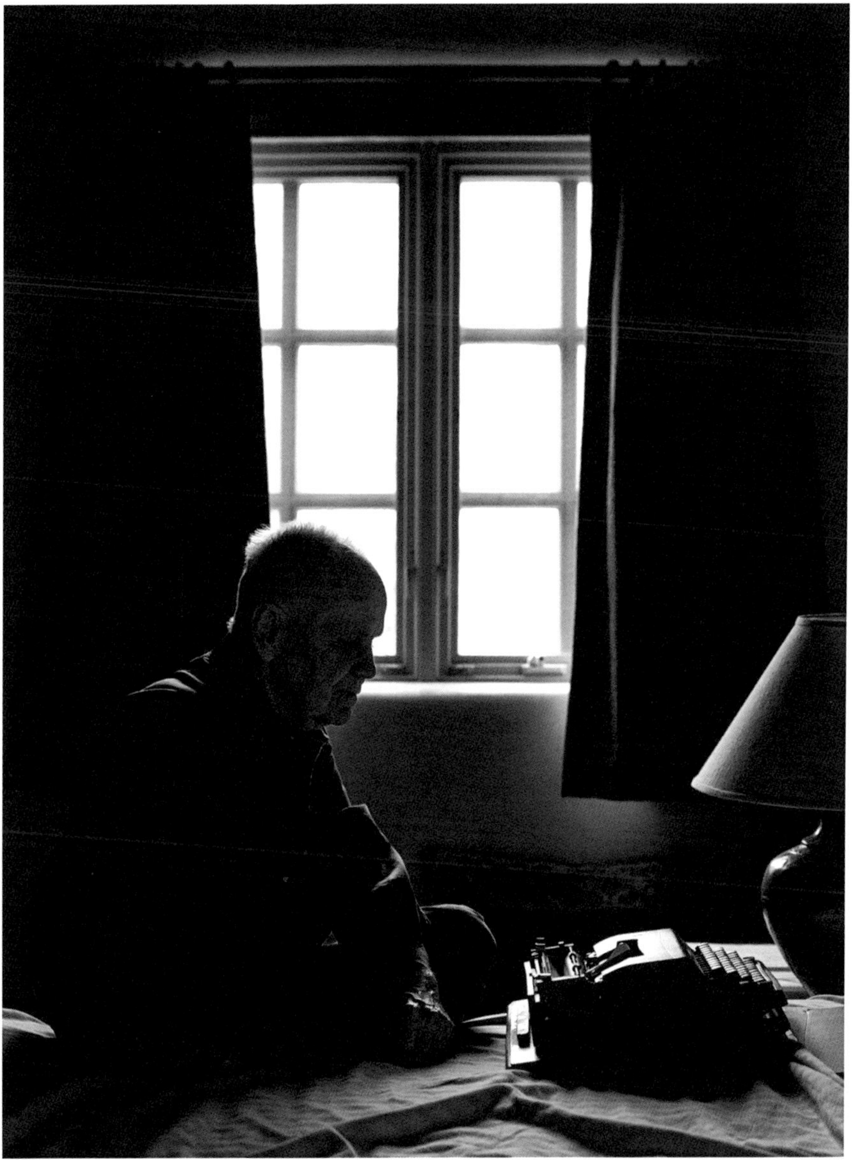

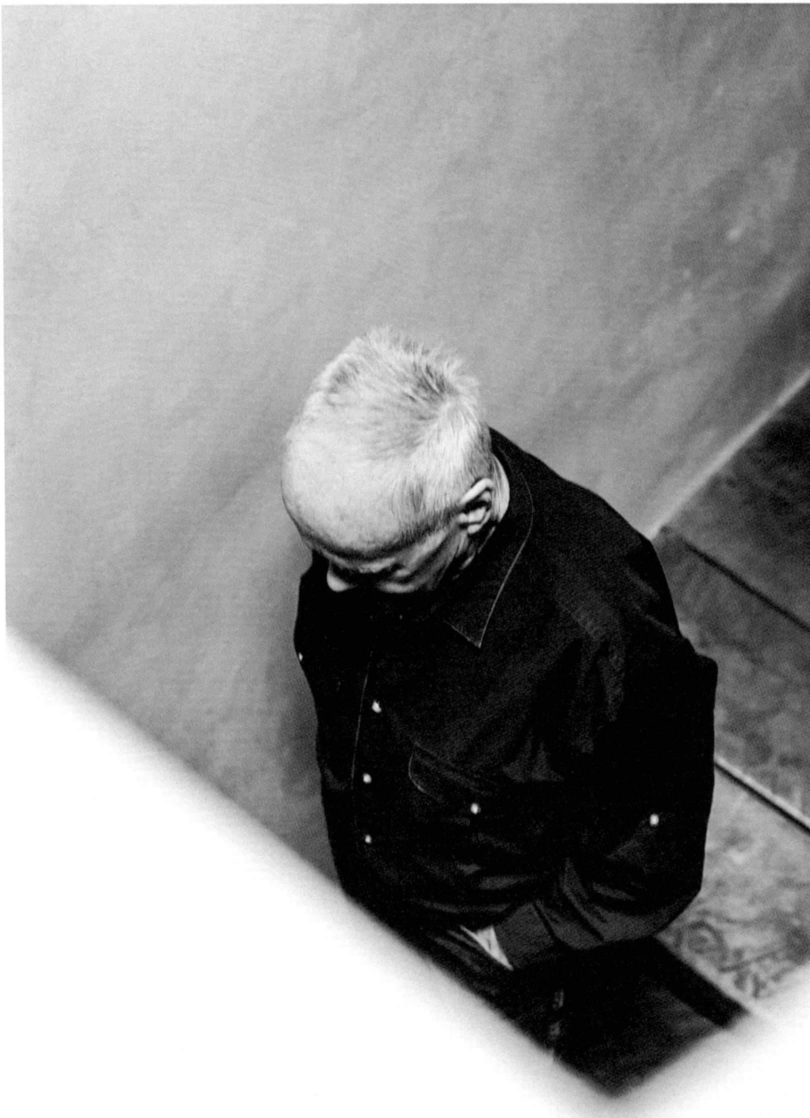

They said that it was no accident of circumstance that a man be born in a certain country and not some other and they said that the weathers and seasons that form a land form also the inner fortunes of men in their generations and are passed on to their children and are not so easily come by otherwise.

—*All the Pretty Horses*

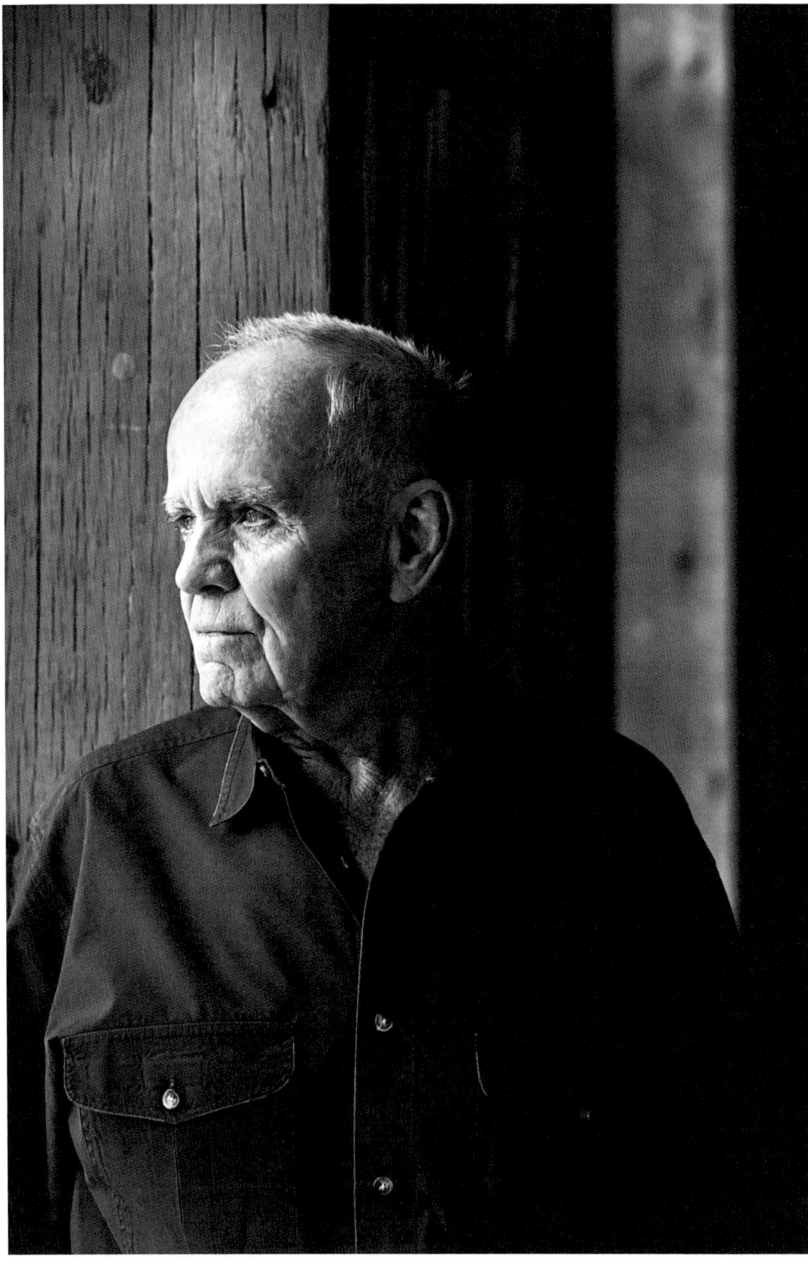

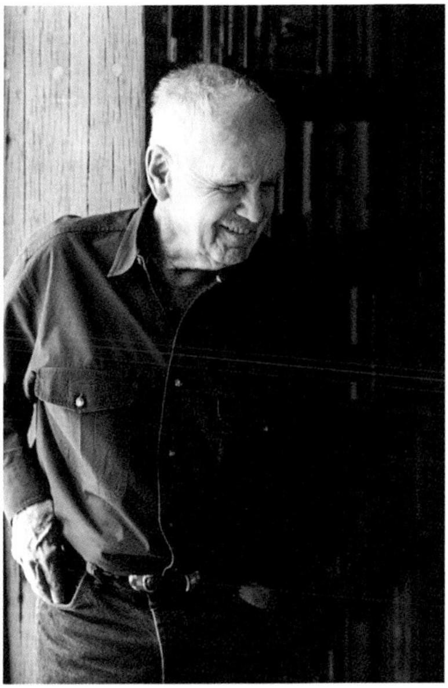
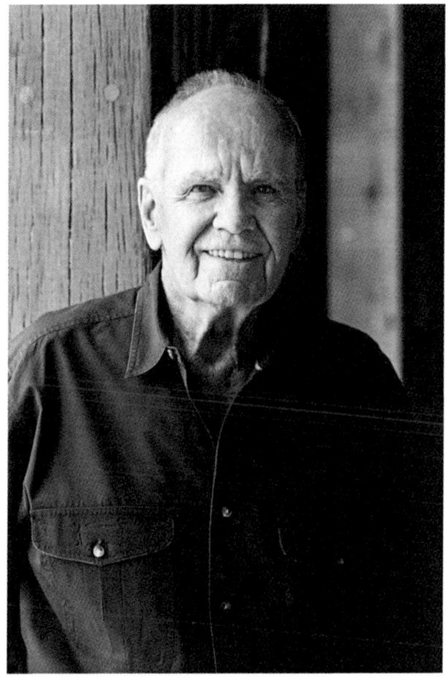
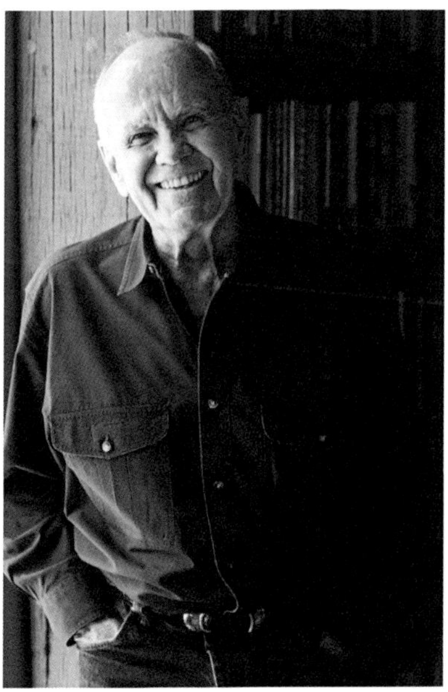
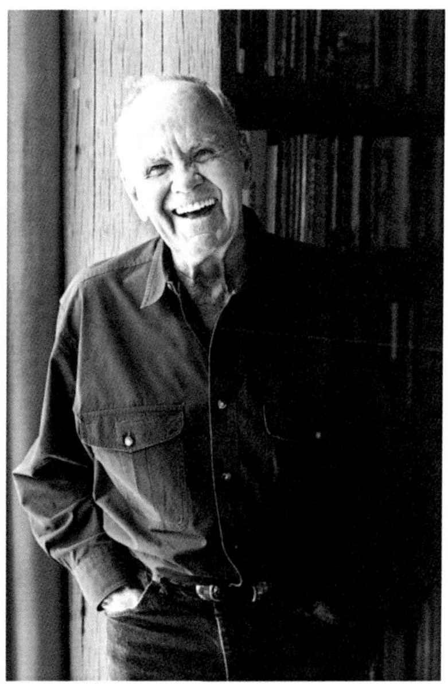

Fathers are always forgiven. In the end they are forgiven. Had it been women who dragged the world through these horrors there would be a bounty on them.

—*The Passenger*

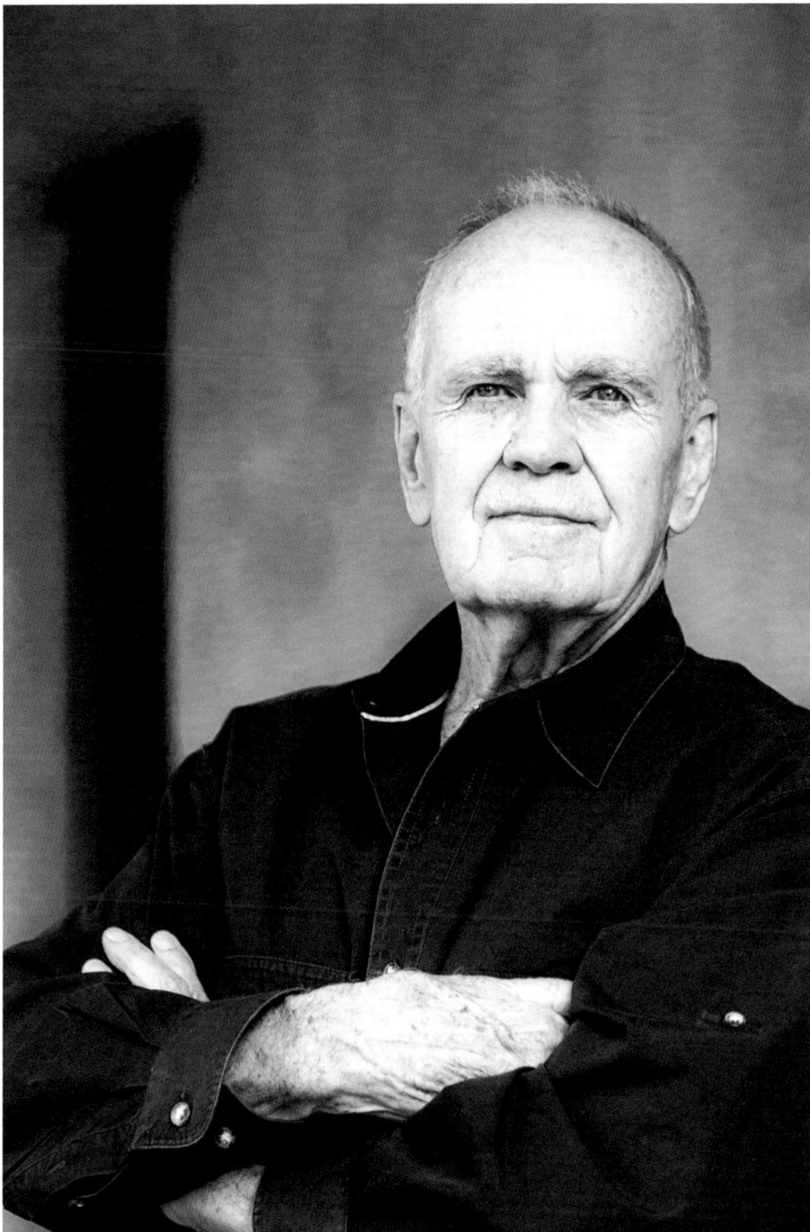

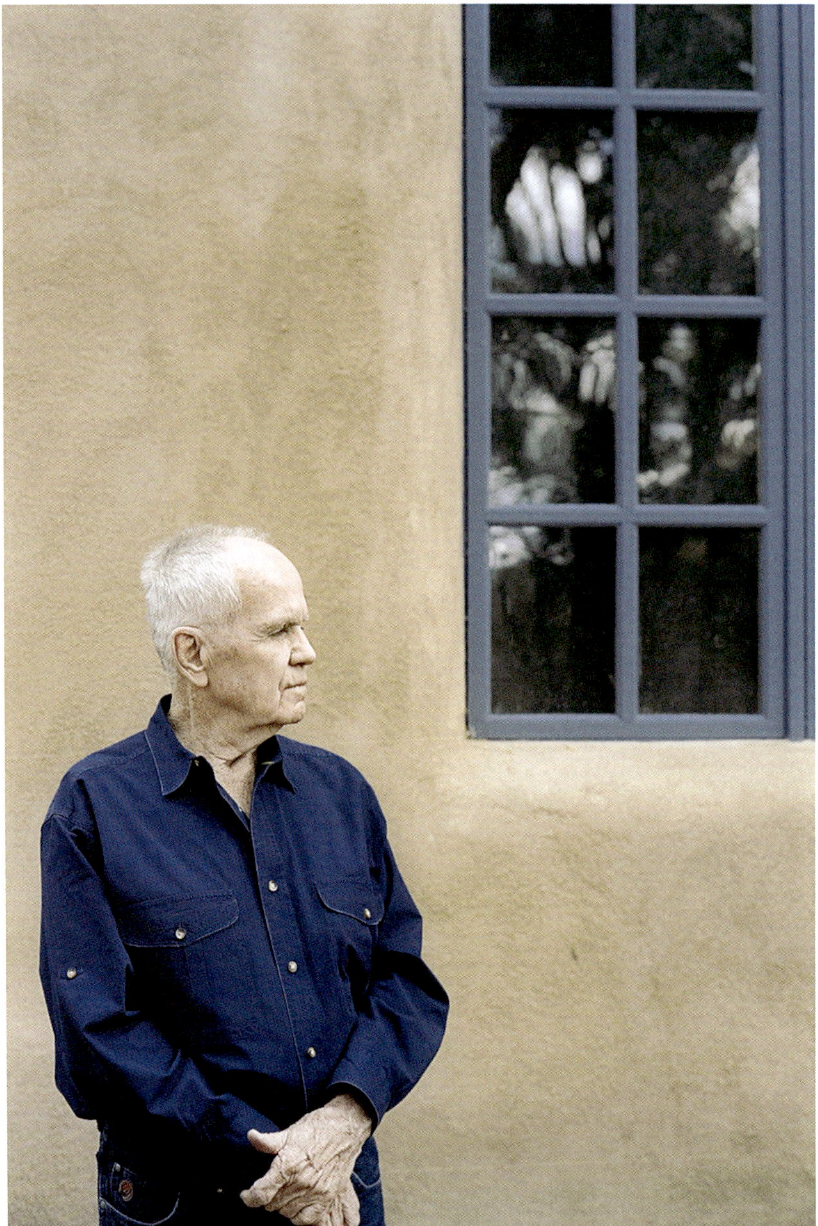

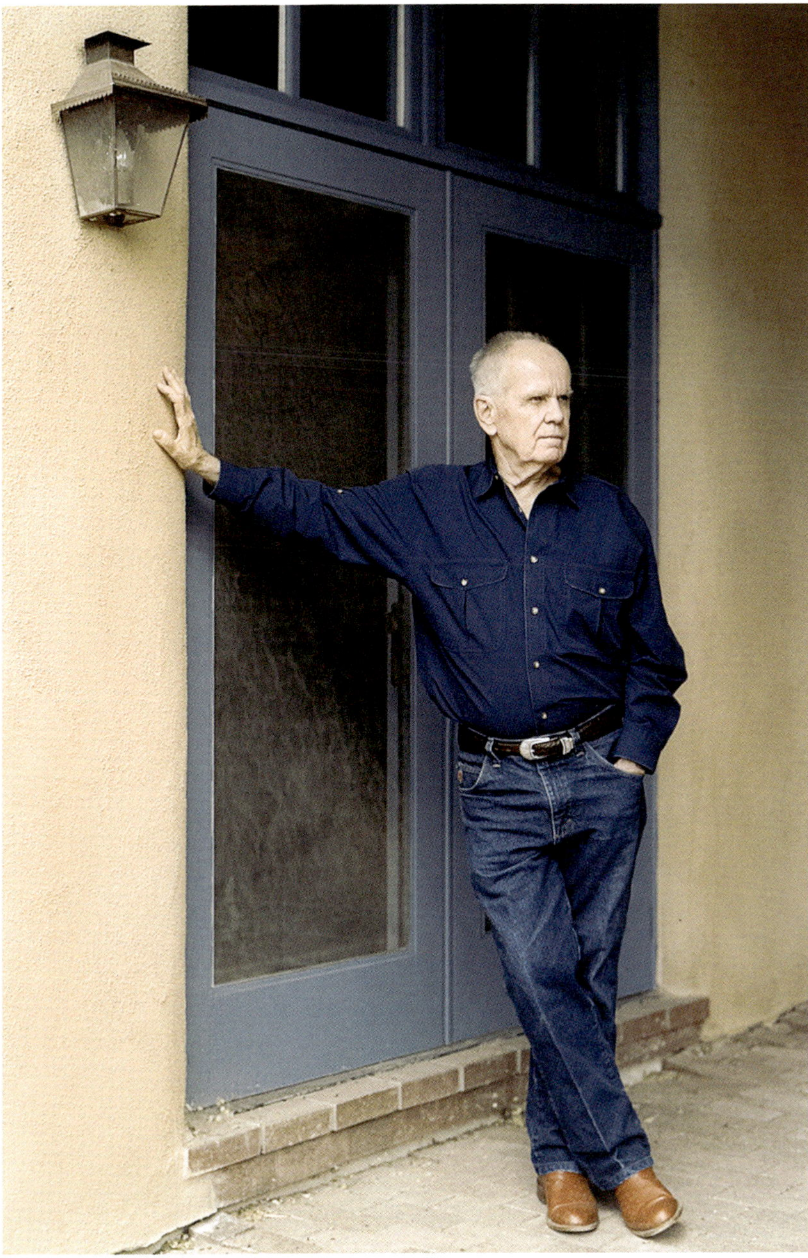

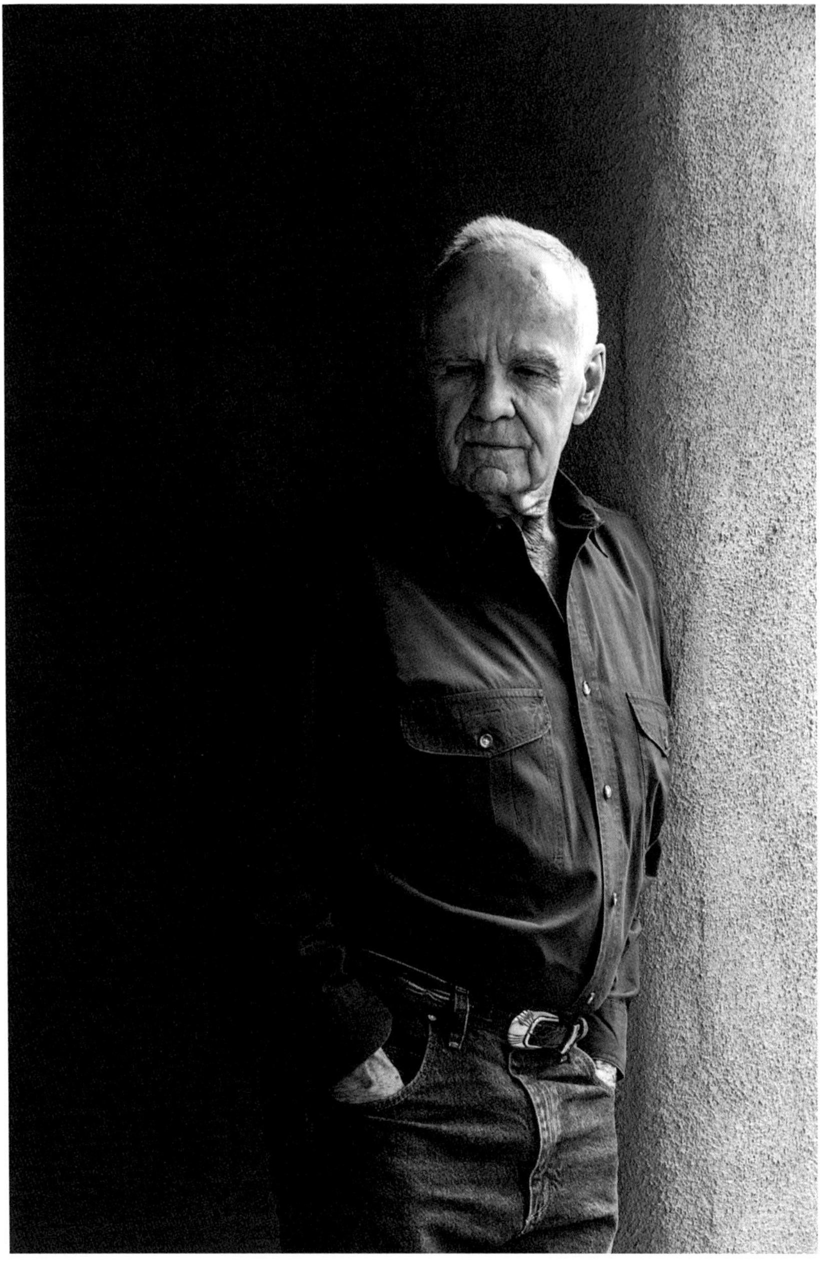

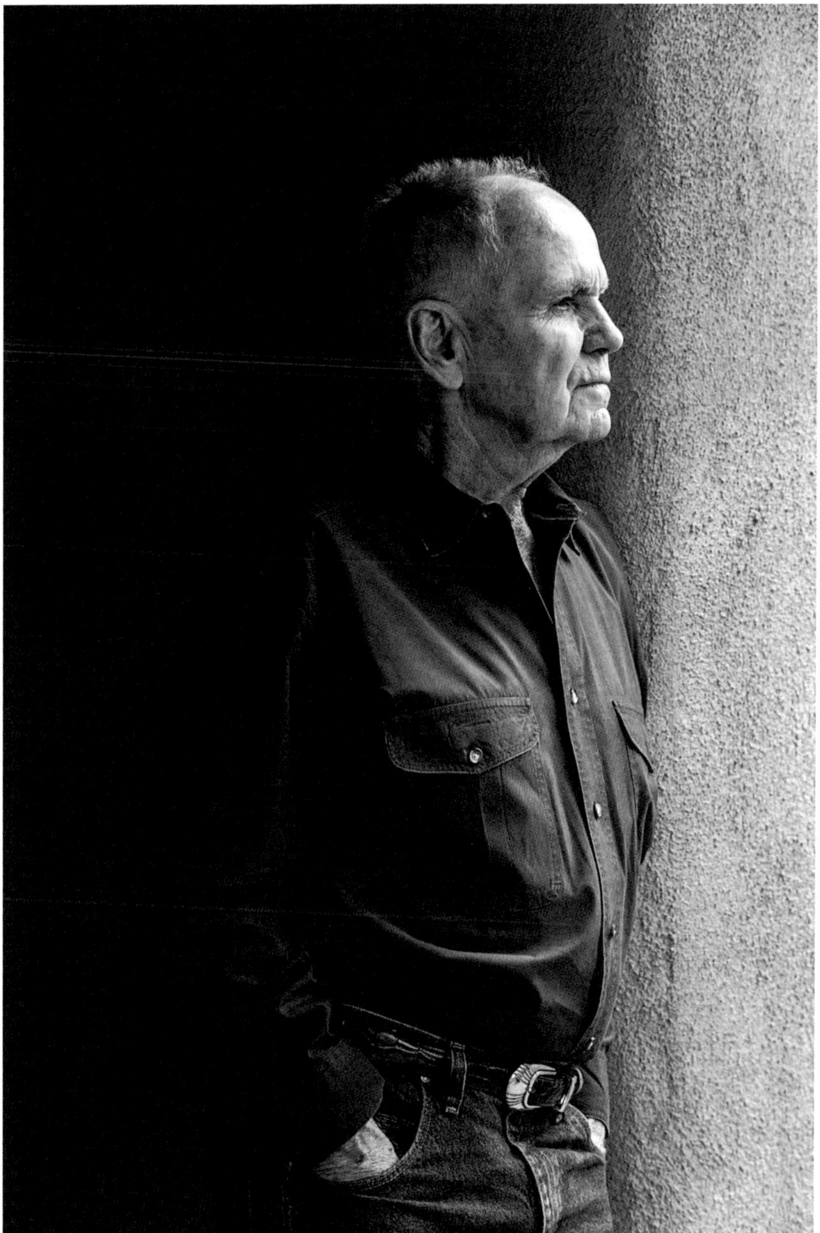

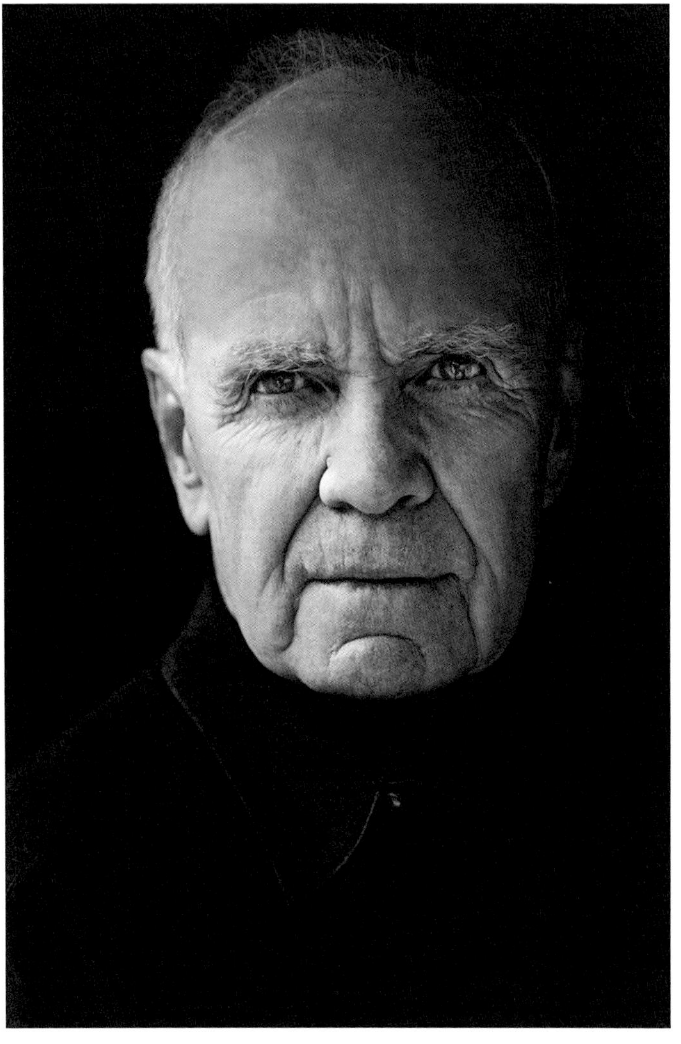

You have to carry the fire.
I dont know how to.
Yes, you do.

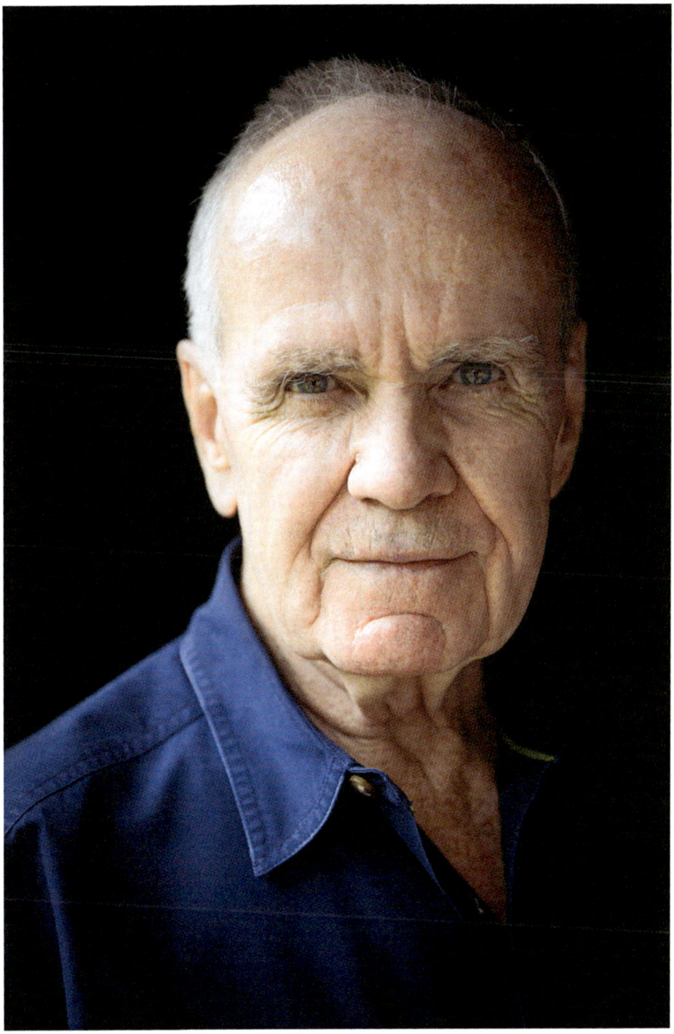

Is the fire real? The fire?

Yes it is.

Where is it? I dont know where it is.

Yes you do. It's inside you. It always was there. I can see it.

—*The Road*

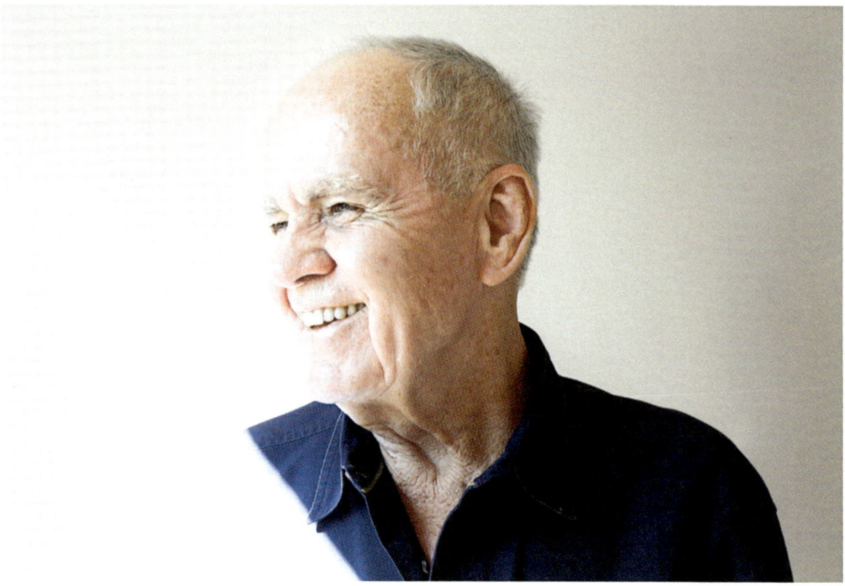

Thursday, September 22, 2022. Near midnight, a car crosses the Williamsburg Bridge and carries me back to Manhattan after a commission out of town. Six hours later, I'm in another car, to LaGuardia Airport, and three hours later in yet another, to the DeSoto Hotel in Savannah, Georgia, where, thanks to an invitation extended by Dr. Stacey Peebles of The Cormac McCarthy Society four months earlier, I deliver the keynote address to the Cormac McCarthy Society Conference. In it, I share with the audience of scholars and fans most of the stories and pictures shared in this book.

Afterwards, many attendees come to say hello or thanks, or to make selfies with me in front of a picture of Cormac beaming behind us on the screen. Soon, an elegantly dressed lady approaches and, with a British accent, asks, "How come Cormac smiled a bigger smile for you than he ever did for me?" I'm disarmed. She says, "I'm Annie DeLisle, Cormac's second wife. Great job." We exchange cards, and she says, with regrets, that she must be on her way.

Later that night, after the joyous closing reception of *The Passenger: Cormac McCarthy by Beowulf Sheehan*, an exhibition at Location Gallery (across the street from the hotel) that Stacey and I had organized with the gallerist Peter Roberts, a few of us walk to dinner. I'm seated opposite Dennis McCarthy, Cormac's brother. An attorney like their father, Dennis is of slender build, taller than his brother. And yet, at least tonight, he's dressed like Cormac. The meter and tone of Dennis's voice, his quiet, kind eyes and face all uncannily like those of Cormac. As we return to the hotel, I observe that Dennis has the same gait as Cormac. "He's my brother," he laughs.

Settled back in my room, I plan to call my own brother. Instead, my phone rings. I don't recognize the number, but the area code is the same as my brother's cell. "Hello, Beowulf, it's Annie. I just wanted to let you know I got home safely and that it was a delight to meet you." The delight was mine, I tell Annie—the surprise of her call was mine, too, but I don't tell her that—and I offer to invite her to coffee when I'm next in her neighborhood. Hanging up, I take it all in. Cormac and I worked together roughly eight years after the publication of *The Road.* In five Tuesdays, a bit more than eight years after our session, *The Passenger* will publish around the world. *Stella Maris* will follow three weeks later. His body of work will be complete. A body of work that pushes us to better see and understand others and ourselves across the spectrum of brutality and beauty. Books that helped me understand my father.

I call my brother. I tell him how well the day celebrating Cormac went. I tell him about the sudden, unexpected call from a number bearing his area code and the lady who made it. He asks her name and proceeds to find Annie on Google. "I know her… She comes to [my daughters'] dance performances. I think she supports the dance company." I reply, "I don't know anything about Annie's marriage to Cormac. But I think her being at the conference must mean she really loved him." My brother answers, "I think that, for all the success Cormac had, a lot of people did."

[ ]

My father passed away April 22, 2018. I was scheduled to photograph Hillary Clinton for PEN America that day. When the news came on the 21st from my brother that our father's time was at hand, I gave my keys and equipment to my assistant Julian (who went on to photograph Clinton). I caught the last flight out of New York for Fort Lauderdale, leaving where my parents met and began their lives together for where my father's life would end. On the morning of the 22nd, I awoke to see him supine, eyes closed, and still breathing.

My father had engaged me with a handshake for most of my life. I countered with a hug the last decades of his. That morning, I could only take his hand as his breathing slowed. I apologized to him, thanked him, forgave him, loved him, and said goodbye. Outside, minutes after my father breathed his last breath, the rain to which I had woken gave way to the sun.

Cormac passed away June 13, 2023. In November 2024, *Vanity Fair* published the story that, at the age of 42, Cormac fell in love with a 16-year-old girl whom he met at a Tucson motel when she asked him to sign her copy of *The Orchard Keeper,* thus beginning a relationship that spanned states and decades. With the news, other elements of Cormac's novels suddenly made sense. In May 2025, I met with Glenn Horowitz, Cormac's archive representative, and broached the subject. "Of course I knew – it was in his letters. They loved each other."

I thought of Annie.

[ ]

Now, in the summer of 2025, my thoughts are of my own story. For multiple reasons that precede my arrival at my building, I must close my home studio of eleven years and soon open another. My neighbors' violence and neglect had grown in recent years, to a level I felt untenable. Doubt, however, creeps in. I put so much into my home. Could I have done more to confront and change those my neighbors so I could stay? Is part of me running? As *Five Easy Pieces*' Bobby Dupea does from his pregnant girlfriend into the passenger seat of a semi-trailer truck? As Bobby Western does in *The Passenger*. As my father did?

Both Bobbys, when asked about their running, answer, "It's all right." In my conference keynote address, I made this connection between both Bobbys and related them to another Cormac line, from *All the Pretty Horses*: "Scared money cant win and a worried man cant love." No. I'm not running. The challenges of my building are greater than my ability to solve them. I did what I could here. It is time. As Platon, the great portraitist and among my beloved teachers, would later say to me, "You have to let go of anything that keeps you from making your art."

I stand on the floor where I sat eleven years ago when I first spoke with Cormac. My maternal grandfather's 1929 Zeiss-Ikon Ikonta camera rests treasured atop my bookshelf. My father's inscription inside his gifted copy of Helmut Newton's *Autobiography* sits steps away. So does his 1972 Polaroid SX-70. My bookplate-signed copy of *The Passenger* is nearby. As I pack, I think of the many wonderful souls I had the honor of photographing here. The love shared among these walls. Storytellers, artists, visitors, mentors, students, family, and friends I'd welcomed from around the world. Moments. Journeys. Girlfriends. Beginnings. Endings. The memory of asking my dad for advice when my heart was first broken. "You can't force a person's feelings… Just say thanks and move on." In moving on, the chance for wonder anew.

Cormac, from *The Road*: "All things of grace and beauty such that one holds them to one's heart have a common provenance in pain. Their birth in grief and ashes."

You have my whole heart.
You always did.
—*The Road*

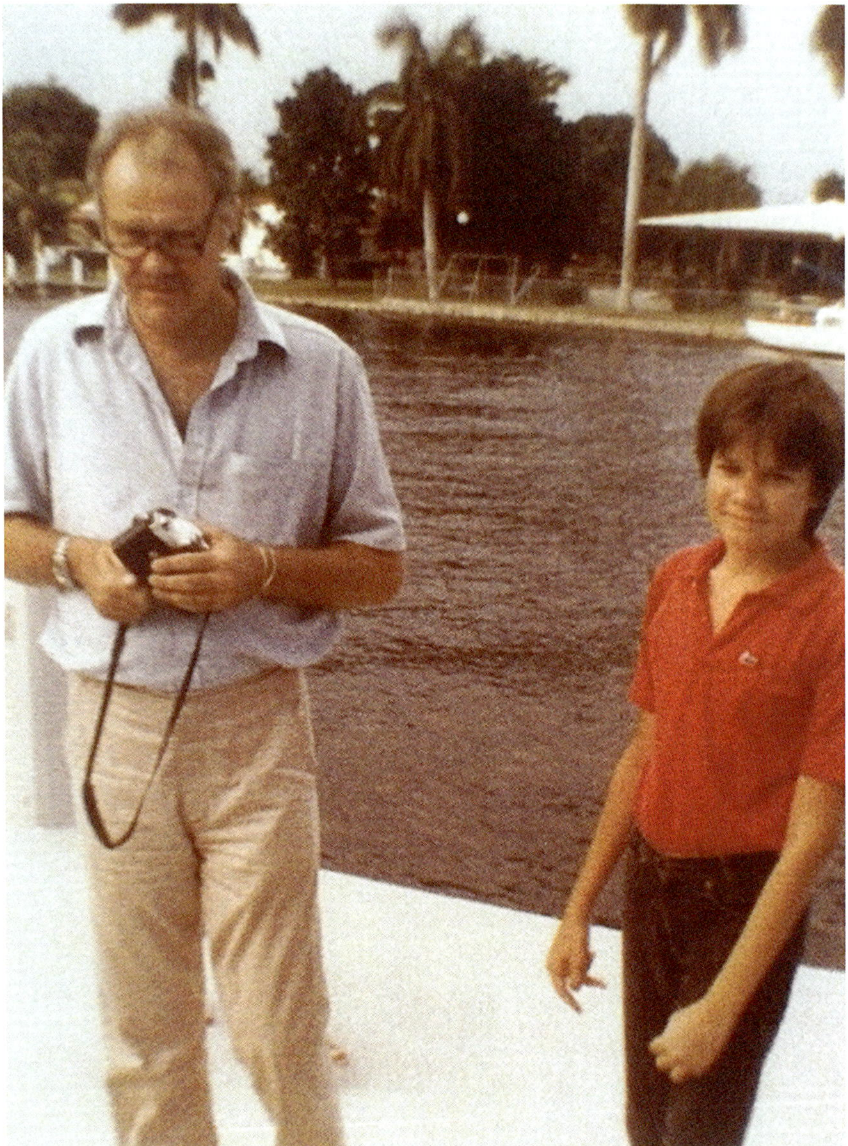

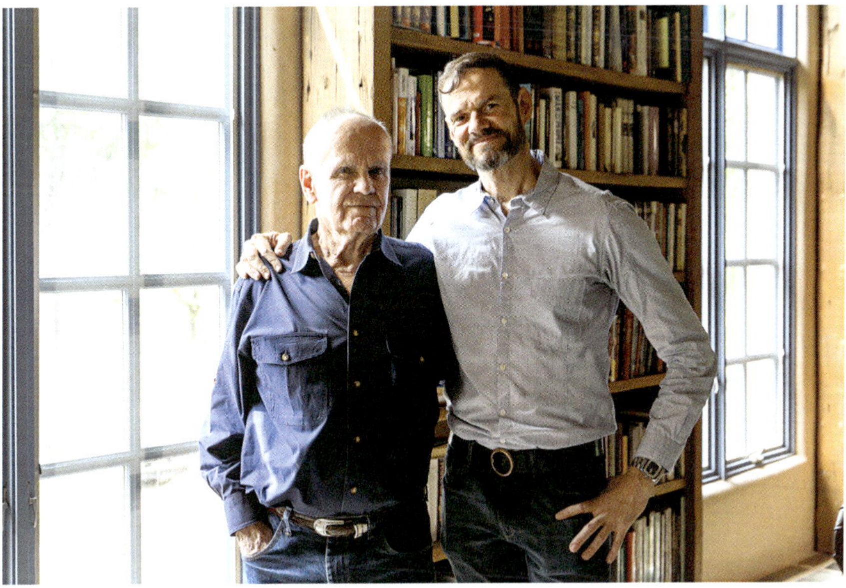

Acknowledgements

My humbled gratitude to Binky Urban, for your faith in me and for opening the door to a day with Cormac and days with other artists of letters you champion.

To Jenny Johnson, Jordan Pavlin, and Nicholas Latimer of Alfred A. Knopf, for your trust that I would serve Cormac, his art, and you well.

To Chika Kobari, for crafting light to make my picture dreams for Cormac come true.

To Eric Simonoff, for believing in a photographer among so many great writers.

To Michael Wheaton of Autofocus Books, for sharing so many stories of art and life. Thank you to David Shields and to you for sharing mine.

To Peter Roberts of Contact Gallery and Stacey Peebles and Steve Frye of the Cormac McCarthy Society, for one of the best days of my life spent celebrating one of the best days of my life.

To Dennis McCarthy and Anne DeLisle, for the warm windows to your hearts. The best of Cormac lives on in you.

To Marion Ettlinger, Greg Gorman, Platon, and Salman Rushdie, heroes turned mentors turned friends, for teaching me how to walk and pushing me to run.

To the advocates, institutions, organizations, publications, and publishers, notably the Authors Guild Foundation, Center for Fiction, Glenn Horowitz, National Book Critics Circle, National Book Foundation, 92NY Poetry Center, PEN America, Story Prize, Windham-Campbell Prizes, Words Without Borders, Black Dog & Leventhal, Farrar, Straus & Giroux, Grove Atlantic, Little, Brown and Company, Macmillan, W.W. Norton & Company, Penguin Random House, Simon & Schuster, champions of literature and free speech here and abroad, and the many storytellers with whom I've had the honor of working, for the chance to celebrate your stories in photographs.

To my maternal grandfather Leopold, for my earliest memories of photography, poetry, and piano, and for the joy ride you inspired.

To my mother Margitta, for your perseverance to love and lift Leif and me, and to my brother Leif, my life-long best friend. How fortunate we are to be here, healthy, grown, and together.

To Dad, Christopher Michael Sheehan, for ultimately embracing my dreams as a loving parent should and, through your challenges, for the chance to love you back. I miss you. At least I get to say hello to you every time I look in the mirror.

To Cormac, for your art to help so many see through darkness both far and near. Thank you for the light of your stories, shone on my father so that I would see him as the man who fought to love Leif and me. And thank you for the light of your kind, open heart in our beautiful day together.

Bibliography

Kushner, David. "'If It Doesn't Concern Life or Death, It's Not Interesting': Cormac McCarthy's American Odyssey," *Rolling Stone,* December 27, 2007.

McCarthy, Cormac. *All the Pretty Horses.* Alfred A. Knopf, 1992.

McCarthy, Cormac. *Blood Meridian: Or the Evening Redness in the West.* Random House, 1985.

McCarthy, Cormac. *No Country for Old Men*. Alfred A. Knopf, 2005.

McCarthy, Cormac. *Stella Maris*. Alfred A. Knopf, 2022.

McCarthy, Cormac. *The Passenger.* Alfred A. Knopf, 2022.

McCarthy, Cormac. *The Road.* Alfred A. Knopf, 2006.

McCarthy, Cormac. *The Stonemason: A Play in Five Acts*. Ecco Press, 1994.

About the Author

Beowulf Sheehan is a photographer of figures in the arts and humanities. To date, he's photographed better than 1,000 writers from more than 60 countries. His work has been published in the likes of *Elle, Esquire, L'Uomo Vogue, The New Yorker, People, Time, Vanity Fair,* and *Vogue* and has been exhibited at institutions such as the American Academy of Arts and Letters, Dostoevsky Museum, International Center of Photography, Museum of the City of New York, Museum of Fine Arts Houston, Smithsonian National Museum of African American History and Culture, and The Witliff Collections. *Author: The Portraits of Beowulf Sheehan*, a collection of portraits of 200 writers from 35 countries with a foreword by Salman Rushdie, was published in 2018. *The Father of the Man: The Last Author Portrait Sitting with Cormac McCarthy* is Sheehan's second monograph. Beowulf Sheehan is the proud son of an immigrant and translator, grandson of a poet and photographer, grandson of a copy editor, first cousin once removed of an editor, and cousin, first cousin once removed, and great-great-nephew of authors. Raised in Fort Lauderdale, Florida, he lives in New York City.

— also from Autofocus Books —

Duplex — Mike Nagel

XO — Sara Rauch

Until It Feels Right — Emily Costa

Cleave — Holly Pelesky

Nextdoor in Colonialtown — Ryan Rivas

Too Much Tongue — Adrienne Marie Barrios & Leigh Chadwick

Picture Window — Danny Caine

the nature machine! — Tyler Gillespie

A Kind of In-Between — Aaron Burch

How to Write a Novel: An Anthology of 20 Craft Essays About Writing, None of Which Ever Mention Writing — ed. Aaron Burch

Hiraeth — Mistie R. Watkins

That Spell — Tate N. Oquendo

My Modest Blindness — Russell Brakefield

A Calendar Is A Snakeskin — Kristine Langley Mahler

Culdesac — Mike Nagel

Razed by TV Sets — Jason McCall

In the Away Time — Kristen E. Nelson

The Body Is A Temporary Gathering Place — Andrew Bertaina

Daughterhood — Emily Adrian

A Healthy Interest in the Lives of Others — Teresa Carmody

Yes I Am Human I Know You Were Wondering — Erin Dorney

Leave: A Postpartum Account — Shayne Terry

Out There In the Dark — Katharine Coldiron

Organic Matter — E.N. Couturier

If I Can Be Honest: Selected Prose from the Four Years of Autofocus Lit (2020-2024) — ed. Michael Wheaton

The Dead Dad Diaries — Erin Slaughter

A Revionist History of Loving Men — Lena Ziegler

Marginalia — Naomi Washer

The Third Beat — Lauren Lavín

Tacoma — Aaron Burch

Teen Queen Training: Essays after The Seventeen Book of Etiquette and Entertaining, 1963 — Kristine Langley Mahler

Disenchanted — Kaycie Hall

What a House Can Hold — Laura Childs Gill

Failure Is the Only Subject: On Documentary Film and a Life Coming Undone — David Shields